THE CIBECUE APACHE

By

KEITH H. BASSO
Yale University

Waveland Press, Inc.
Prospect Heights, Illinois

For more information about this book, write or call:

Waveland Press, Inc.
P.O. Box 400
Prospect Heights, Illinois 60070
(312) 634-0081

Cover photograph: Girl's puberty ceremonial.

For my grandmother

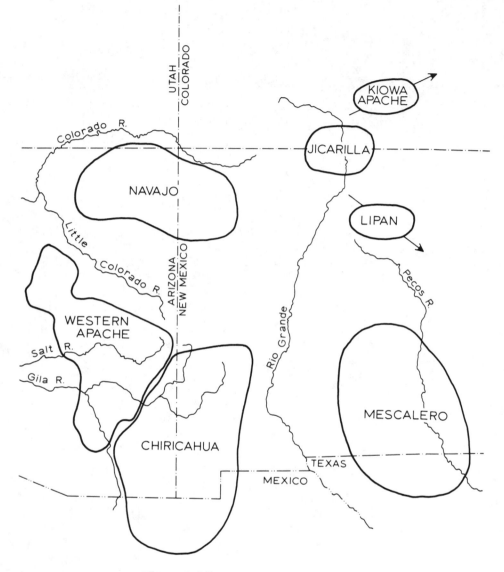

Figure 1. The major groups of Apacheans.

Foreword

This is a study of an American Indian community that has retained its cultural character. The Apache of Cibecue have not survived unchanged from their turbulent past, but they maintain premises about the way the world is, revealed in belief and behavior, which are sharply divergent from those of the majority population of North America.

Keith Basso communicates the character of Apache culture to the reader in two major ways: (1) through objective analysis and description; and (2) by letting the people speak for themselves. In both ways, however, he never strays far from the Apache reality. He classifies the twenty-eight different kinds of power that can be acquired through purchase and with prolonged instruction. He provides an exact analysis of the attributes of the witch as conceived by the people. He describes step by step the girl's puberty ceremony and details its meaning and functions. In each area of belief and behavior he isolates generalizable features, but also provides descriptions of real behavior in specific situations and verbatim statements by the people themselves. One never loses sight of the fact that the people of Cibecue are alive, now, and that Basso has set for himself the goal of describing *their* perception of events as well as organizing *his* perception of their behavior into a structured statement relevant to the concerns of the social scientists. This combination makes for compelling reading, both from the standpoint of the student of anthropology and from that of the reader interested in American Indians in general, the Southwest and its history, or the Apache in particular.

Although the author's main concern is with the Apache world as the Apache perceive and think about it, he also provides, in the first two chapters, a very useful treatment of their social organization in pre- and post-reservation times—as ordered by the anthropologist. Two possible definitions of the anthropologist's task are thus illustrated in this study: either to analyze the cultural system on the an-

v

thropologist's terms, or on the native's terms. Both strategies have their uses, and a modern ethnography should, we think, include both.

Readers familiar with the nature of anthropological fieldwork will understand what went into Keith Basso's work in Cibecue. He learned the language well enough to use it as the major means of his communication in the field. He became a friend of the people, living as much as he could as they did. He was a participant observer in the most meaningful sense that this term is used by anthropologists; a friend and intimate, but always as well an observer motivated by intellectual concerns that he could never fully share with his friends, and armed with research techniques that evolved out of a totally separate cultural tradition than the one he studied in the field. And his participant observation did not consist of a happy summer or two spent in Cibecue. He began his fieldwork, at Clyde Kluckhohn's suggestion and under his initial direction, when an undergraduate at Harvard, and he has continued it, for substantial periods of time each year, up to the present. For these reasons this study is a "close up" of Cibecue Apache life.

GEORGE AND LOUISE SPINDLER

Preface

Linguistically related to Athapaskan-speaking peoples in Alaska, Canada, and northern California, the Southern Athapaskans, or Apacheans, were intrusive to the American Southwest. Prehistorians place the time of their arrival in this area at between A.D. 1000–1500, but the exact route they traveled and the chronology of their migrations has not yet been precisely determined.

After they entered the Southwest, the Apacheans separated into several smaller groups which, by the late 1500s, had spread over a vast and varied region extending from central Arizona to northwestern Texas. In the centuries that followed, these groups, now relatively isolated from one another, adapted to local ecological conditions (including the presence of other tribes) and developed the linguistic and cultural characteristics that distinguished them in historic times. On the basis of these characteristics, anthropologists have divided the Apacheans into seven major tribes: the Jicarilla Apache, the Lipan Apache, the Kiowa Apache, the Mescalero Apache, the Chiricahua Apache, the Navaho, and the Western Apache (see Figure 1 [frontispiece]). This book is about the Western Apache, not as they lived in the past—although this will concern us—but as they survive today in Cibecue, a small settlement on the Fort Apache Indian Reservation in east-central Arizona.

Although far-reaching changes have occurred since the establishment of reservations in the 1870s, it would be a serious mistake to suppose that traditional Western Apache culture has been completely lost or eradicated. The twentieth century Apache thinks of himself as an Indian. And well he might. The language he learns first, and the one he prefers to communicate in, is still Western Apache. Grammatically complex, it embodies a large number of concepts—some quite abstract—for which English offers no ready equivalents. When he is learning his language, the Apache is trained in accordance with established practices of child-care that differ conspicuously from our own. As an adult, he enters a social world that generates tensions and holds out rewards quite unlike those characteristic of American society. Finally, and perhaps most importantly, he acquires a view of the universe grounded in assumptions about natural phenomena, the capabilities of men, and the manipulation of supernatural entities that contrasts sharply with the standard tenets of Western ideology and philosophy.

Clad in denim pants, shirts, boots, and wide-brimmed hat, the modern Western Apache is capable of giving the impression that he has adjusted fully to his new place in the society and economy of the American Southwest. No doubt there will come a time when this is true. But it has not yet arrived.

The primary aim of this book is to describe portions of the Western Apache belief system, especially those which deal with what members of Western society might call "religion" or "the supernatural." We shall see, however, that many of these beliefs, together with the ritual activity predicated upon them, cannot be understood independently of the groups which compose Apache society. Therefore, it will be necessary to begin with a discussion of social organization.

At the heart of Western Apache religion are the alliances that obtain between men and supernatural "powers." Because powers develop qualities—one is tempted to say personalities—that are highly individualistic, each Apache who "owns" one is likely to portray it as unique. Much of what Apaches assert about themselves and their environment is marked by a similar kind of personal bias. One learns, however, that beneath this layer of diversity there is a set of concepts about the nature and composition of reality which almost all Apaches hold in common. I have generalized about some of these, but at the same time—aware that such generalizations are at best the approximations of an outsider—I have allowed my informants to speak for themselves. They, after all, are the authorities on Western Apache culture.

To portray the culture of the Cibecue Apache as something fixed and immutable would be dangerously misleading. It has changed considerably in recent years, and is destined to change even more. Rather than simply document this process, I have tried to indicate some of the ways in which it effects the lives of individuals. The members of any society whose culture is in flux are likely to experience conflict and indecision. This is as true of twentieth-century Western Apaches as it is of ourselves.

Since 1960, I have spent nearly twenty-five months on the Fort Apache Reservation. All but a small portion of this research was financed by generous grants from the National Institute of Mental Health and the United States Public Health Service. I am very grateful for this support.

At one time or another, earlier versions of chapters in this book were read by Charles Frake, Morris Opler, Benjamin Paul, George Spindler and Evon Z. Vogt. I thank them for their comments and criticism.

I would also like to express my gratitude to the Office of Anthropological Research, Washington, D.C., for permission to reprint the figures which accompany Chapter 5; the University of Arizona Press for permission to reprint Figures 1, 2, and 4, and the University of New Mexico Press for permission to quote from Charles R. Kaut's *The Western Apache Clan System: Its Origin and Development*. Finally, I want to thank Tad Nichols of Tucson, Arizona, for the photograph which serves as the cover illustration.

* * * *

Now I sure want to say something to those people in Cibecue. Long ago, we had trouble talking and I did not know if you wanted to talk to me. But you did and you taught me good things. I sure don't know them all yet, but that doesn't make a difference. We both tried to understand.

KEITH H. BASSO

Pronunciation Guide

Western Apache words and phrases are written in accordance with the phonetic orthography presented below. In the interests of simplicity, vowel length, stress, aspiration, and tone have not been indicated.

Vowels
a, as in English father
æ, as in English bat
e, as in English met
i, as in English bead
ɩ, as in English hit
o, as in English mow
u, as in English boot
ɔ, as in English claw
ə, as in English but
ɛ, a diphthong, as in English may

Vowel nasalization is indicated by a subscript hook, for example a.

Consonants
b, voiced bilabial stop
t, voiceless alveolar stop
d, voided alveolar stop
k, voiceless velar stop
g, voiced velar stop
n, voiced alveolar nasal
m, voiced bilabial nasal
č, voiceless alveopalatal affricative
ǰ, voiced alveopalatal affricative
s, voiceless alveolar fricative
z, voiced alveolar fricative
š, voiceless alveopalatal fricative
ž, voiced alveopalatal fricative
h, voiceless glottal fricative
l, voiced alveolar lateral
ł, voiceless alveolar lateral (usually spirantal)
w, voiceless bilabial semivowel
ʔ, the glottal stop

Contents

THE CIBECUE APACHE

Apache girl dressed for cere-monial, Cibecue 1961.

Apache man, Cibecue 1962

Apache boy, Cibecue 1962

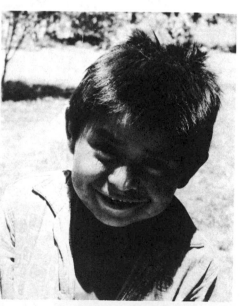

1

Pre-Reservation Western
Apache Society

IN ORDER to understand how the Western Apache live today, it is essential to have some idea of how they lived prior to the establishment of reservations. Therefore, this chapter is devoted to a summary of Apache society as it existed before 1870. We shall draw heavily on the work of Grenville Goodwin whose massive ethnography, *The Social Organization of the Western Apache*, contains a wealth of information on pre-reservation life and provides a detailed background against which to assess the forces that have altered Apache society during the past century.

Goodwin (1935:55) designated as Western Apache: ". . . those Apachean peoples who have lived within the present boundaries of the state of Arizona during historic times, with the exception of the Chiricahua Apache and a small band of Apaches, known as the Apache Mansos, who lived in the vicinity of Tucson." The totality of people thus designated—Goodwin estimates that between 1850 and 1875 there were approximately 4000—were divided into five subtribal groups that occupied contiguous regions in the eastern and central portions of Arizona (see Figure 2).

The White Mountain Apache, easternmost of the Western Apache groups, ranged over a wide area bounded by the Pinaleño Mountains on the south and by the White Mountains to the north. To the southwest, in the foothills of the Santa Catalina Mountains and on both sides of the San Pedro River, lived the San Carlos Apache. The territory of a third group, the Cibecue Apache, extended north from the Salt River to well above the Mogollon Rim; its western boundary was formed by the Mazatzal Mountains, homeland of the Southern Tonto Apache. The Northern Tonto, which of all the Western Apache groups lay the furthest west, inhabited the upper reaches of the Verde River and ranged north as far as the present community of Flagstaff.

1

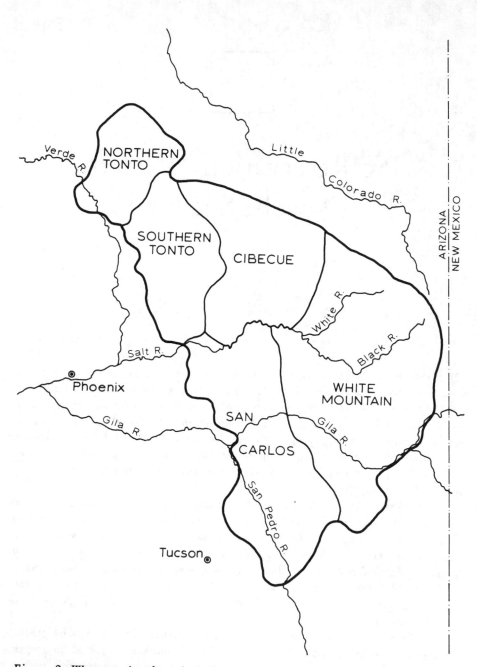

Figure 2. Western Apache subtribal groups.

All together, the Western Apache occupied a territory of nearly 90,000 square miles (Getty 1964:27). Characterized by extreme ecological diversity, it is a region of jagged mountains and twisting canyons, of well-watered valleys and arid desert. Elevations rise from 2000 feet above sea level to slightly less than

12,000, and temperatures fluctuate from near zero in the winter to well above 100 degrees during the months of July and August. Precipitation ranges from about ten inches at the lower elevations to twenty or thirty at the higher altitudes. The flora varies considerably, from essentially desert types, including a large number af cactus species, to heavy stands of conifers, cottonwood, and oak. Game in the form of deer, elk, wild turkey, javelina, and bear is plentiful.

In pre-reservation times, contact between the Western Apache groups and surrounding peoples was fairly regular. Small-scale trading was carried on with the Hopi and Zuni to the east and with the Yavapai to the west. Relations with the Navaho, intermittently friendly and hostile, were always fraught with suspicion. The Pima and Papago, enemies of long standing, were the targets of continual raiding, as were the frequently defenseless Mexican farmers scattered throughout southern Arizona and northern Sonora and Chihuahua. On the whole, dealings with the Chiricahua were amicable until around 1870 when Western Apache men enlisted as scouts and, at the head of U.S. Cavalry columns, helped hunt down renegade Chiricahuas who had fled the reservations.

Although the Western Apache engaged in subsistence farming, their economy was based primarily on the exploitation of a wide variety of natural resources by hunting and gathering. Goodwin (1937:61) estimates that agricultural products made up only 25 percent of all the food consumed in a year, the remaining 75 percent being a combination of meat and undomesticated plants. Because they could not rely on crops throughout the year, the Western Apache did not establish permanent residences in any one place. In fact, except for early spring, when there was planting to be done, and early fall, the time of harvest, they were almost constantly on the move.

In May, the people deserted low-altitude winter camps in the Salt and Gila River valleys and trekked overland to farm sites in the mountains. Here they seeded small plots (generally about a half-acre in size) of corn, beans, and squash. Once this was finished, large gathering parties set out in search of sahuaro fruit, the prickly pear, and the Apache staple: mescal. Older people unwilling to make the trek, the disabled, and a few children remained behind to cultivate the fields.

Acorns and mesquite beans were collected in July and August, and by September the fruit of the Spanish bayonet (yucca) was ready for picking. In the early fall the Apache returned to their farm sites, harvested their crops, and spent most of October and November gathering piñon nuts and juniper berries. As the food was brought in, it was either eaten on the spot or stored in baskets for the months ahead. Hunting was best in the late fall, and it was not until a good supply of game had been secured that the people headed again towards their winter camps, thus completing the annual cycle.

In pre-reservation days a significant portion of the Western Apaches' meat supply consisted of stolen livestock. Although raiding parties made occasional forays into Navaho country in search of sheep and goats, most predatory action was directed toward southern Arizona and northern Mexico. Here, in the vicinity of small Mexican communities and settlements of Pima and Papago, the Apache could steal large herds of horses (which they used for food as well as transportation), burros, mules, oxen, and cattle. Once captured, the animals were driven north and taken to mountain strongholds where their recovery, even by large numbers of armed pursuers, was made extremely difficult.

Besides livestock, the members of raiding expeditions sometimes returned home with captive women and children. In most cases they were not maltreated. Women prisoners were expected to work hard, and those who did so ungrudgingly were considered a definite asset. Similar demands were made of child captives, and so long as they did not attempt to escape they were accorded many of the same privileges as Apaches their own age.

Unlike raiding activities, for which a desire for livestock provided the chief incentive, war parties were carried out solely to avenge deaths suffered at the hands of an enemy. The maternal relatives of a slain warrior played the major role in organizing a war party and generally composed the bulk of it. Plans for such expeditions were invariably the same: return to the spot where the death had occurred; track down the men responsible; and then—usually in carefully executed early morning ambush—kill as many as possible.

Prior to the establishment of military posts in the late 1860s, and actually for quite some time thereafter, the Western Apache were able to carry out their raiding and warring activities with virtual impunity. Elusive and resourceful, they possessed remarkable powers of endurance and a complete knowledge of the terrain they sought to defend. Together with the Chiricahua, they presented the last major obstacle to the settlement and exploitation of the Southwestern frontier. General George Crook (21st Infantry), who was probably the Apaches' greatest admirer as well as the man most responsible for bringing about their defeat, described them as the finest light cavalry in all of North America.

Social Organization

The cultural anthropologist, Robert Lowie (1947:1), has defined social organizations as "the groups into which society is divided, the function of these groups, their mutual relations, and the factors determining their growth." Ralph Linton (1945:56-57), on the other hand, maintains that "formulations of social structure must begin at the other end of the sociocultural continuum. They must show how the individuals who compose society are classified and organized, since it is through these mechanisms that the society's members, as individuals, are assigned their roles." As Pospisil (1964:398) points out, these two definitions refer to two distinct realities: to the groups which comprise society and their interrelationships; and to individuals and the ways in which they structure their dealings, through roles and statuses, with other members of their society.

In discussing the Western Apache we shall keep the two definitions separate. Following Pospisil's (1965:399) suggestion, the term *social structure* will refer to "the cultural ordering of Ego's relations with other members of his society." To the nature and interrelations of society's segments we shall assign the term *social organization*. The remainder of this chapter will focus on Western Apache social organization, because it is in this sphere that reservation life has produced the most far-reaching changes. Social structure appears to have altered comparatively little and will be treated less extensively.

Although the five Western Apache subtribal groups—the Cibecue, San Carlos, White Mountain, and Northern and Southern Tonto—intermarried to a limited degree, they considered themselves quite distinct from one another. Open conflict between them was not uncommon, and they never formed anything like a unified political entity. The territorial boundaries of each group were clearly defined, and it sometimes happened that trespassers were forcibly expelled or killed.

Each subtribal group was divided into from two to four *bands*. According to Goodwin, band distinctions were not as marked in some subtribal groups as in others, but each had its own hunting grounds and, except when pressed by starvation, was reluctant to encroach upon those of its neighbors. Using military censuses, it is possible to compute a mean size for Western Apache bands between 1888 and 1890. This figure comes to 387 individuals, but there was considerable variation in both directions. For example, the San Carlos band of the San Carlos subtribal group had only fifty-three members, whereas the Eastern White Mountain band of the White Mountain group numbered 748. Although bands were characterized by an internal unity somewhat greater than that of the subtribal group as a whole, they did not participate in any form of joint political action. As Goodwin (1935:55) puts it: "Bands were units only in the sense of territorial limitations and minor linguistic similarities."

Bands were composed of what were unquestionably the most important segments of pre-reservation Western Apache society, what Goodwin referred to as *local groups*. In his words "these were the basic units around which the social organization, government, and economic activities of the Western Apache revolved" (Goodwin 1942:110). Each local group had exclusive rights to certain farm sites and hunting localities, and each was headed by a chief who directed collective enterprises such as raiding parties, food-gathering expeditions, farming projects, and activities involving other local groups and tribes.

Local groups were made up of from two to six *gota* or, in Goodwin's terminology, *family clusters*. In most cases, the family cluster was no more than a large matrilocal extended family, that is, three to eight nuclear households, each of which had at least one female member who was a descendant or sibling of an older woman in the group. There were exceptions, however, because in spite of a prevailing tendency for married men to take up residence in their wives' family cluster, it was not unusual for a son—particularly an only son—to remain with his mother and sisters and bring his wife to live with them.

The persons who constituted the matrilineage that formed the core of a family cluster shared membership in the same clan (see Figure 3). This is noteworthy because a family cluster, unlike local groups and bands, was not designated by territorial location but by the clan of its core lineage. Thus, Goodwin (1942: 128) writes: "The Apache readily identifies a family cluster by its nuclear clan and will often say, 'The people in that cluster are of such and such a clan,' although in fact it may be composed of members of several clans . . . by mentioning the nuclear clan of the unit he emphasizes the primary bond holding it together."

Western Apache of the San Carlos group. Date of photograph is unknown, but it was probably taken in the 1870s. (Courtesy of the Western History Collections of the University of Oklahoma Library and the Arizona State Museum.)

Alchesay, famed White Mountain Apache chief. Photograph was taken in 1930. (Courtesy of the Western History Collections of the University of Oklahoma Library and the Arizona State Museum.)

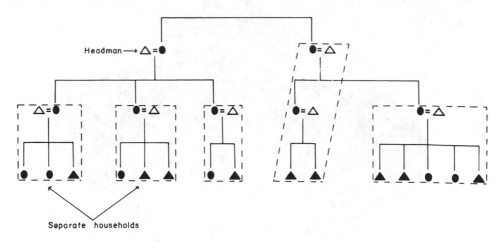

Headman ⟶

Separate households

Figure 3. Schematic diagram of Western Apache family cluster.

A considerable amount of endogamy occurred within the local group and, in fact, this seems to have been the desired arrangement. Kaut (1957:63–64) gives what is probably a sound explanation:

> Basically, people who had grown up in the same area could operate together as a better economic team. Matrilocality required that the woman remain in the area to which she had been educated in terms of farming and gathering activities. Gathering activities, especially, required a very specific knowledge of rough terrain which could only be gained over a period of many years. The man's main economic activities were centered around hunting and raiding, which also required extensive training and integration into a tightly organized group. A man hunted best on his home ground, both because he knew it so well and because he garnered power from the very ground itself—a power which he lost when he entered other hunting grounds. He was trained for war and raiding by his mother's parents, his father, his elder brothers, and his mother's brothers. . . . For these reasons, a local group composed of extended families which drew their members from the same general area could operate more efficiently than one which contained many men who were strangers to its hunting territory. . . .

Each family cluster was under the leadership of a headman. Although he might be a member of the cluster's nuclear clan, the headman was more often an outsider, a relative by marriage. At first, a man who married into a family cluster worked for his wife's parents and found himself more or less at their complete disposal. However, as he gained authority and developed the qualities necessary for leadership, his status was reversed and, "his wife's relatives lived with him, not he with them" Goodwin's (1942:131).

On the initiative and advice of their headman, the members of a family cluster undertook farm labors, set forth on small-scale food gathering expeditions, and moved camp. In addition, headmen were called upon to discuss prospective marriages and help settle disputes that arose between family clusters within the local group. Skill and success in the arbitration of such disputes was highly esteemed, and it was primarily on this basis that local group chiefs were chosen from among the ranks of family cluster headmen.

It was customary for headmen to lecture their family clusters early in the morning. The speeches usually concerned everyday matters and were directed at all within earshot. The following is a typical example.

Do not be lazy. Even if there is a deep canyon or a steep place to climb, you must go up it. Thus, it will be easy for you to get deer. If any of you go out hunting this morning, tomorrow, or the following day, look after yourselves while you are alone. When you trail deer you may step on a rock. If the rock slips from under you, you may fall and get hurt. If there is a thick growth of trees ahead of you, don't go in it. There might be a mountain lion in a tree ready to attack you. Always go on the upper side or the lower side of such a clump. If there is thick brush ahead, there may be a bear or some wolves in it. Go above or below it. When you trail a deer and you come upon him, if he should start to run, don't run after him for a deer can run faster than you, and you cannot overtake him. You women who go out to gather acorns and walnuts, don't go alone. Go in a party of three or four. Look after each other. If you get a mescal head ready to cut off, don't stand on the lower side of it; always work on the upper side. If you stand below it while you cut, it will roll on you, and its sharp points will stick into you. If you cut it off and are about to chop away the leaves from the head, don't open your eyes wide. Close them halfway so the juice won't get in them and blind you (Goodwin 1942:166).

The Western Apache clan system is best considered separately from bands, local groups, and family clusters. Whereas these latter units were spatially distinct, clans were not. Members of the same clan were scattered throughout Apache country, thus creating an extensive and intricate network of relationships that cut across bands and local groups, but at the same time served to join them together. The members of a clan considered themselves related through the maternal line, but they were rarely able to trace the genealogical links involved. This is not surprising when it is understood that the Apache thought of a clan as being composed of the descendants, not of a common ancestor, but of the group that established the first agricultural site with which the clan was associated. Each clan had a name which referred to this legendary place of origin. All told there were sixty-two clans.

Marriage between members of the same clan was not countenanced, although marriage into the father's clan was permissible and, there is some evidence to suggest, even preferred. Persons belonging to the same clan were expected to aid each other whenever possible, and if it was deemed necessary the entire clan might be called upon to avenge a wrong done to one of its members. However, beyond these obligations, and the important but somewhat restricted influence of clan chiefs, there was little in the way of formal clan government or law. The clan's main functions were to regulate marriage, extend obligatory relationships beyond the extended family, and facilitate concerted action in projects requiring more manpower than was available in the family cluster or local group.

All but a few of the sixty Western Apache clans claimed affiliation to one of three archaic clans and, on this basis, were grouped into phratries (Kaut

1957:40). A phratry was composed of clans which, in Apache terms, were either "closely related," "related" or "distantly related" (see Figure 4).

A single clan was "closely related" to from two to ten others. The members of closely related clans were not allowed to marry and were bound by reciprocal obligations only slightly less demanding than those between persons of the same clan. Closely related clans formed an exogamous segment—called a *section* by Goodwin—which related to all other clans as a unit. In other words, with regard to one another, as well as to clans outside their section, closely related clans shared identical marriage restrictions.

"Related" clans belonged to separate sections, but were nonetheless bound by ties almost as close as those between clans in the same section. Marriage was prohibited, and mutual obligations were strong. With respect to other clans, however, two sections of related clans rarely observed the same marriage restrictions. For example, one section (A) might be related to another (B), which in turn might be related to a third (C). The relationship between A and B did not necessarily imply a corresponding relationship between A and C. As Kaut (1957:41) puts it, "the term 'related' merely signified a bond of obligation and marriage restriction between two separate groups of 'closely related' clans or sections."

"Distant relationship" between two clans or sections generally meant that each was "related" to a third clan in common. The members of distantly related clans were permitted to marry and were less constrained by obligations of mutual support.

It is important to remember that persons belonging to the three types of clans lived in local groups spread throughout the whole of Western Apache territory. By establishing obligations of kinship among these individuals, the phratry system bound them together, and in so doing probably helped to keep in check divisive tendencies inherent in local group isolation. It also provided the primary means of recruiting participants for activities—such as raiding parties

Figure 4. Schematic diagram of Western Apache phratry.

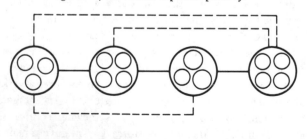

○ Single Clan

Clan Section (composed of closely related clans)

——— "Related" sections

- - - - "Distantly Related" sections

and extensive ceremonial undertakings—that required the cooperation of large numbers of people. Thus Kaut's (1957:41) observation that "the phratry in its relations with other phratries formed a close approach to tribal organization."

An appreciation of the importance of clan and phratry in pre-reservation times may be gained from the following passage, which was taken from Goodwin's unpublished field notes, and consists of the observations of an Apache who was born shortly before 1860.

Over at Ash Flat where I was born, I used to live. This was before the White soldiers came to Goodwin Springs (1864). When I was growing up, my mother told me I had many relatives from all over this country, but I guess I didn't think about it. Then, when I was six years old, my mother's brother, a chief, got sick and died. It was winter when he died, but right away everyone from around the camp where we lived came to the place where he died. Some of those people said: "We should bury this man right away." But then some other people said: "No, it is not right to bury that man now. Right now, in places far from here, his relatives are getting ready to come here. We should wait to bury him so his relatives can see him." Right then I didn't think many people would show up. But the next day some came.

In the morning, just at dawn, some *iya'aiye* came in. These people were of my uncle's clan, my clan. First there were some men on horses and, after that, women. They were walking and carrying baskets with food. When they came close, one of those *iya'aiye* men said: "My brother is dead now so we have come to see him." After that, on the same day, many people came from the north. Some of these were *iya'aiye,* but mostly they were *kiya'an* and *tu'agaidn*. (Note: these two clans are in the same phratry with *iya'aiye*).

Pretty soon there were lots of people there. Many I had never seen and some of the men looked mean and made me afraid. I told my mother but she said: "No, don't be scared. Those people are your relatives and that is why they have come here. Even though they are not living with us, they have come to help us out. They know we are sad and they have brought us food to eat."

The next day some other people came—maybe 100 of them. There were *iya'aiye* with them but most of them, I think, were *dzltadn* and *tlukadıgaidn*. These clans are related to *iya'aiye* (i.e., belonging to the same phratry). They wanted to see my uncle and so they all went over to where he was. Three of those woman began to cry and yell. "Our brother is dead, has gone away." Like that. They yelled it over and over.

After my uncle was buried, all those people stayed at Ash Flat for two days. They helped make food for our people who lived there. Then they went back to their own camps. Some had a long way to go. After that, I knew I had relatives from all over this country. I saw many of them after I grew up. It was that way. If someone was in trouble or needed help his relatives would come a long way to help him out. And he would try to do that for them.

Social Structure

In his book, *The Social Organization of the Western Apache*, Grenville Goodwin presents a detailed discussion of kinship terminology, together with a large body of information concerning the behavioral norms that governed inter- action among kinsmen. The picture of Western Apache kinship given here is a simplified one and, as such, is apt to convey a misleading impression of neatness. Nevertheless, it should give some insight into the basic considerations that underscored the classification of kinsmen, as well as the kinds of behavior expected of persons occupying critical kinship roles.

In the parental generation, Ego's father and mother are separated terminologically. Father's siblings are classed together regardless of sex, but mother's sister and mother's brother are labelled by distinct terms. This classification may be represented as follows:

	šima	šita	šimaʔa	šitaʔa	šibeže
+1 Gen	Mo	Fa	MoSi	MoBr	FaSi; FaBr

In Ego's own generation siblings are differentiated according to sex, and sibling terms are extended to parallel-cousins. Separate terms are used for cross-cousins. Thus:

	šila	šikisn	šilaʔaš	šizege
0 Gen	Si; FaBrDa; MoSiDa	Br; FaBrSo MoSiSo	FaSiSo MoBrSo	FaSiDa FaSiSo

In the generation immediately below Ego's own, sons and daughters are distinguished from brother's children and sister's children, and the latter two are distinguished from one another.

	šiyεʔ	šitsiʔ	šidaʔa	šibeže
−1 Gen	So	Da	SiDa; SiSo	BrDa; BrSo

Maternal grandparents and their siblings of both sexes are grouped under a single term (šičo), whereas paternal grandmother and her sisters (šičıne) are differentiated from paternal grandfather and his brothers (šindale). Grandparent terms are applied to grandchildren. Thus, the children of Ego's daughter are designated šičo, and those of his son šindale.

The importance of the clan and phratry in Western Apache social structure is suggested by the fact that kin terms denoting close biological relatives were extended to all phratry members, even though their exact genealogical relationship to Ego might be unknown. Thus, clan and phratry members of Ego's generation were classed with siblings, those of the parental generation with siblings of Ego's mother, and those of the second ascending generation with maternal grandparents. Persons in the first descending generation were classified as children of Ego's sister.

Terms for relatives acquired through marriage (affinals) were distinct from those applied to blood relatives (consanguineals). Ego's mother-in-law and father-in-law were classed together (šaʔadni), as were grandparents-in-law and spouse's siblings (šiʔi). There was a single term for any man marrying a blood relative and another for any woman marrying a blood relative.

In describing kinship behavior we shall make reference to three factors that Goodwin considered critical:

1. *Authority.* Although Goodwin does not define exactly what he means by authority, he uses it in the following sense: an influence possessed by an individual, but not necessarily backed by the threat of coercion, which causes another individual to conform to the former's decisions or requests.

2. *Obligations.* Two types are distinguished: reciprocal obligations, which are symmetrical in that the demands upon A with respect to B are identical to those of B with respect to A; and nonreciprocal obligations, which are asymmetrical is that A has obligations to B, but B has none toward A (or vice-versa).

3. *Restraint.* Social relations among the Western Apache were (and still are) marked by differing degrees of restraint. The latter, which the Apache interpreted as a sign of respect, prohibited familiarities such as joking and touching, and in some cases resulted in almost complete avoidance. Relationships characterized by the absence of restraint were considerably more relaxed, unattended by any of the restrictions mentioned above, and might involve an institutionalized form of joking. In general, restraint was displayed in the presence of persons in authority, whereas its absence typified interaction between persons of approximately equal status.

The strongest reciprocal obligations existed between Ego and the members of his matrilineage (see Table 1). Especially binding were those with his mother's sister, his mother's brother, siblings, and maternal parallel cousins. These individuals were expected to cooperate with one another at all times, protect each other's interests, and share surplus food and material goods. Except for Ego's father, reciprocal obligations with paternal kin were weak. According to Goodwin (1942:157), "they were not directly interested in the individual, and therefore their relationship to him did not carry with it the common interests shared by members of the same matrilineage and clan."

Authority over Ego was primarily in the hands of his father and his mother's brother. The close bond with a maternal uncle was particularly important for a boy, who regularly turned to his mother's brother when in need of serious counsel. The fact that the uncle often lived in another family cluster did not matter.

Social relations with parallel cousins and siblings of the opposite sex as Ego were typified with restraint, as were dealings with his father and all maternal kinsmen of the first, and second ascending generations. Cross-cousins, automatically of a clan other than Ego's, were not bound by strong reciprocal obligations and frequently carried on a joking relationship. To a lesser extent, this also appears to have been true of paternal grandparents.

Nowhere was restraint more pronounced than in relationships with affinal kin (see Table 2). Parents-in-law had direct authority over their daughter's husband, and until he showed himself to be a good provider he was obligated to perform any task they requested. Reciprocal obligations were absent. The strictest

TABLE 1
KINSHIP BEHAVIOR (CONSANGUINEAL KIN)

Kin Type	Possesses Authority over Ego	Restraint	Obligations
Mo	+	+	S
Fa	+	+	S
Mo Parents	+	+	S
MoBr	+	+	S
MoSi	+	+	S
Siblings	—	+	S
Matri. parallel cousins	—	+	S
Patri. parallel cousins	—	—	W
Matri. cross cousins	—	— (j)	W
Patri. cross cousins	—	— (j)	W
FaBr	—	—	A
FaSi	—	—	A
Fa Parents	—	— (j)	A

S = strong reciprocal obligations
W = weak reciprocal obligations
A = absence of reciprocal obligations
(j) = joking relationship

TABLE 2
KINSHIP BEHAVIOR (AFFINAL KIN)

Kin Type	Possesses Authority over Ego	Restraint	Obligations
WiMo	+	+ (a)	NR
WiFa	+	+	NR
WiMoBr	+	+	A
WiMoSi	+	+	A
WiSi	—	+	A
WiFaSi	—	—	A
WiFaBr	—	—	A
WiBr	—	—	A

NR = nonreciprocal obligations
A = absence of reciprocal obligations
(a) = avoidance relationship

avoidance and respect were in force between a man and his mother-in-law. They could not touch each other or sit in the same dwelling, and under normal circumstances were not permitted to address each other except through an intermediary. A man's relationships with his wife's parents could be extremely onerous and frequently gave rise to feelings of hostility which, if the proper respect was to be maintained, had to be suppressed.

This brief description reveals very little of the complexities of Western Apache social life, but it does highlight the central role played by matrilineal kin. These were the individuals to whom an Apache turned for support, who trained and directed him until he reached adulthood, and who provided him in times of crisis with solace and the assurance of loyalty and support. As noted earlier, the local group, the matrilineage that formed its core, and the clan were the most important segments of Western Apache social organization. We have tried to suggest here that these same groups were equally critical in ordering the individual's social relations—in assigning him roles, in structuring his expectations of others, and in establishing relatively fixed guidelines for the organization of his own behavior.

Marriage

Clan exogamy, together with restrictions prohibiting the marriage of close paternal kin, were the most significant factors governing the selection of spouses. Goodwin (1942:311) reports that on rare occasions persons belonging to "related" clans married, as did paternal parallel cousins. However, such unions were criticized as incestuous, and were thought to result eventually in the deaths of the individuals involved.

In pre-reservation times and during the early reservation years, a few men had more than one wife. Goodwin recorded twelve polygynous marriages from the period before 1880, and in all of these the men were either chiefs or persons of considerable wealth. The overwhelming majority of marriages were monogamous. Polygynous unions were usually with women of the same clan, and it was not uncommon for a man to marry a pair of sisters.

Divorce appears to have been fairly common and was easy to obtain. There was nothing to prevent husband or wife from marrying again, sometimes almost immediately. According to Goodwin (1942:343), accepted grounds for divorce were ". . . laziness, incompetence, or unwillingness to perform expected tasks . . . failure of a man to observe respects and avoidances with his wife's kin . . . continual quarreling . . . maltreatment of a wife, unreasonable jealousy, and infidelity." Most divorces apparently followed upon protracted quarrels, at which time either the husband or wife gathered up his essential belongings and, after announcing his intentions never to return, walked off.

Religion

Most published studies on the Western Apache have been concerned with the description and analysis of social organization and social structure. So pervasive has been this interest that information about beliefs and activities which could be labeled "religious" is very incomplete. Consequently, no summary of pre-reservation religion is possible.

There are scattered references to "religious concepts" in Goodwin's *Social*

Organization, but unfortunately these do not add up to anything approaching an adequate description. We have a representative collection of Western Apache myths (Goddard 1919, 1920; Goodwin 1939), a tentative classification of ceremonials (Goodwin and Kluckhohn 1945), and an account of one Apache's participation in a nativistic cult (Goodwin and Kaut 1954). The single most valuable source is Goodwin's paper, *White Mountain Apache Religion.* Published in 1938, this brief article presents a highly condensed outline of "shamanism and ritual" among one of the five Western Apache subtribal groups.

With the possible exception of descriptions given in Bourke (1892) and Reagan (1930), available accounts of Western Appache ceremonials fall well below contemporary anthropological standards. Nonetheless, it is abundantly clear that reservation life has brought about marked changes in organized ritual activity. Ceremonies relative to warfare, hunting, childbirth, agriculture, boys' puberty, and traveling have passed out of existence. However, a wide variety of diagnostic and curing ceremonials, together with the girls' puberty rite, are still performed with regularity (Basso 1966).

Almost nothing has been written about witchcraft. Goodwin mentions some of the uses of "love magic" in his *Social Organization,* and a fascinating account of a witchcraft trial appears in one of the tales he collected (1939:144). But here the matter rests.

2

Post-Reservation Western Apache Society

I N THE 1870s, after more than twenty years of bitter conflict with Mexican and U.S. troops, the majority of Western Apache were settled on the Fort Apache and San Carlos Indian Reservations in east-central Arizona. It is significant that the area covered by these reservations was also Apache territory during aboriginal times because, unlike so many American Indian tribes, the Western Apache were never forcibly uprooted and permanently removed from their original homeland. Many Apaches are living today exactly where their ancestors did decades and centuries before. This has enabled the people to retain a profound sense of identification with the land, its farm-sites, its ceremonial dance-grounds, and has undoubtedly contributed much to the continuity of a cultural tradition which, in certain of the more isolated settlements, has withstood the forces of change with remarkable resilience.

There have been changes, however, and some of major consequence. Old distinctions between bands and local groups have broken down and, as noted previously, the ceremonial system has been depleted. The imposition of a cash and credit economy, the adoption of Western technology, forced adherence to a legal system the principles of which most Apaches do not understand, obligatory attendance at government schools, and an increasing number and variety of missionaries—all have produced alterations in the aboriginal pattern.

Cibecue

The following description of contemporary Western Apache society is based on material gathered in the settlement of Cibecue, located near the center of the Fort Apache Indian Reservation a few miles south of the Mogollon Rim

17

Figure 5. Map of Arizona showing location of Fort Apache Reservation.

(see Figure 5). Established in 1870, the Fort Apache Reservation covers 1,664,872 acres and is the home of approximately 5000 Apaches, most of whom are descendants of the White Mountain and Cibecue subtribal groups. The Indian population is distributed fairly evenly among nine exogamous settlements, six of which —Whiteriver, Canyon Day, East Fork, North Fork, Seven-mile, and Turkey Creek —are located within a ten-mile radius of one another at the eastern end of the Reservation. The other three communities—Carizzo, Cedar Creek, and Cibecue— are situated in valleys to the west and are considerably more isolated.

According to Goodwin (1942:23) the first peaceful relations between Whites and Apaches living in the Cibecue region occurred in 1857 when the Indians received word that a group of Americans (whether or not they were soldiers is not known) wished to meet with them at a spot in the Canyon del Oro on the western side of the Santa Catalina Mountains near Tucson. At first, fearing treachery, the Apaches were reluctant to make the journey, but after deliberating they decided to go. The Americans gave away calico, copper wire for bracelets, and corn. They also made talk of lasting peace.

When Camp Grant was established on the San Pedro River in 1859, a few of the Cibecue Apache drew rations there. But it was not until ten years later, when a military post was founded at what is now Fort Apache, that they obtained rations regularly. In 1875, a large number of Apaches were moved from the Cibecue region to the reservation at San Carlos where they were compelled to remain for several years. Most of them returned to the present settlement of Cibecue and, in 1881, engaged in the historic "Cibecue Massacre" during which a number of U.S. Cavalry troops were killed while attempting to arrest an Apache medicine man. As far as can be determined, this encounter marked the end of overt hostilities with the military.

In 1893 there were thirteen local groups in the Cibecue area with a combined population of 943 (Goodwin 1942:97). The groups were located in three distinct ecological regions, which are in fact separate drainages arising in the Mogollon Plateau. Each group occupied its own valley, and during most of the year operated independently of neighboring groups. Collectively, the local groups within each region comprised what Goodwin termed a "band." These were: the Canyon Creek band, with five constituent local groups; the Carizzo band, with four; and the Cibecue proper, also with four.

After the conflict in 1881, a subagency was established in Cibecue, and all the local groups in the surrounding territory began to settle near it. A trading post was built, and it was not long before Cibecue started to take the place of the old winter camps on the Salt and Gila Rivers. With the opening of a school and the enforcement of regular attendance, the old pattern of "wintering below" ceased entirely, and people from Canyon Creek and Carizzo set up permanent residence in and around Cibecue. In this way, the distinctions between bands and local groups were blurred and then obliterated, and the modern "community" or settlement had its genesis.

The settlement of Cibecue is located at an altitude of 4940 feet, in a shallow mountain valley walled by low sandstone buttes and bisected longitudinally by Cibecue Creek, a narrow stream originating in springs to the north. Apache camps, marked by wickiups, small wooden shacks, and separated by farming plots which vary greatly in size, are strung out on both sides of the creek for a distance of nearly 5 miles. Some of the camps are connected by narrow dirt roads (virtually impassable in wet weather), but the majority are linked by footpaths and horse-trails. Cibecue has two privately owned trading posts and two schools, one of which is run by the Lutheran Apache Mission, the other by the Bureau of Indian Affairs. A government-sponsored "community building" was erected in 1963, and a saw-mill, which for some undefined reason is forever breaking down, began operations in 1965. Over the years missionaries of five outside faiths—Catholic, Lutheran, Mormon, and two fundamentalist sects—have built churches. There is also a small police court and a two-cell concrete jail.

Food-gathering activities in Cibecue are now undertaken primarily in the spirit of family outings, and reservation-imposed hunting seasons greatly restrict the hunting of big game. In the late 1950s it appeared as though farming was on

View of Cibecue valley looking south, 1968.

Typical Apache camp, Cibecue 1968.

Gathering acorns, Cibecue 1968.

Typical Apache wickiup (recently abandoned), Cibecue 1968.

Butchering beef, Cibecue 1963.

a decline, but it has subsequently flourished with renewed vigor. In 1965 well over sixty fields of corn were planted, ranging in size from a half-acre to an acre and a half. A few families have started vegetable gardens which, in addition to beans and squash, may contain tomatoes, carrots, and even a few rows of sugar-cane. The amount of agricultural produce is not large, however, and for the majority of families it constitutes only a minor supplement to purchased foods.

The modern economy revolves around individual wage earnings, income from cattle sales, trading post credit, and Government subsidies in the form of wel-fare checks and social security benefits. Until recently, jobs were very hard to come by in Cibecue, but the sawmill and the construction of a new school are currently providing employment for about thirty men. Five or six others work regularly as cowboys in the Cibecue, Oak Creek, and Grasshopper cattle districts, and this number is swelled to as many as fifteen during roundups. Three Apaches are in the employ of the Forestry Service, and between six and ten work as trading post clerks. There are two Indian policemen stationed in Cibecue and one reservation game warden. Two men work as janitors at the Bureau of Indian Affairs' school, and another helps maintain the irrigation system. However, unemployment is still a major problem, and it is a safe estimate that at any given time there are between twenty-five to thirty able-bodied men who, either because of personal preference or the scarcity of jobs, are out of work.

When large families must be continually fed and clothed, cash wages go only so far. The extension of credit at trading posts helps relieve the situation somewhat, but it also serves to keep the Apache in perpetual debt. He is prevailed upon each month to make small payments on his bill, but frequently, owing to more pressing demands, this is impossible. When he falls too deep "in the hole" further purchases may be denied him except on a strict cash basis. Money is not plentiful in Cibecue, and only a very few individuals—with steady jobs and a sizeable number of cattle—have a surplus of funds.

In pre-reservation times most economic activities were collective enter-prises, carried out by relatively large groups of people working together. This is no longer the case. The introduction of Western economy has emphasized to a degree heretofore unknown the productivity—that is, earning power—of the individual. This, together with the passage of legislation which effectively removed the ownership of land from clans and placed it in the hands of individuals, has resulted in several significant changes. The most far-reaching of these has un-doubtedly been the emergence of the *gową*, or nuclear household, as a primary economic unit and the decline in this capacity of the family cluster.

Social Organization

The Apache term for Cibecue valley is *desčibɩko* ("red canyon, standing horizontally"), and the 850 people who live there are called *desčibɩko nde* ("people of red canyon, standing horizontally"). Another term, *ła dagota* ("many family clusters") is sometimes used to designate the settlement as a whole, but more commonly refers to a group of family clusters (*gota*) related by clan or through traceable consanguineal ties.

Western Apache cowboys (1960). (Courtesy of the Arizona State Museum.)

Whites have partitioned Cibecue into "upper" and "lower" divisions, but these are essentially arbitrary and bear little or no relation to those considered important by the Apache themselves, who designate sections of land along Cibecue Creek according to the historical origin of the people who live there. The largest of these sections in terms of both acreage and population is called čən čon ("thick feces"). The forebears of the people living there were indigenous to Cibecue valley and, according to legend, were among the first to establish farms. These, it is said, were so productive that their owners had more than enough to eat and, as a consequence, their excrement was unusually large. Hence the name čən čon. Further north, on the eastern side of the creek, is an area called gulkɨžn ("spotted land"). Apaches from the Canyon Creek band settled here, and the term gulkɨžn refers to the juniper dotted country from which they came. North of gulkɨžn are two smaller sections whose inhabitants, like those of čən čon, are said to be descended from local groups in the original Cibecue band. One of these is called dzɨłtadn (literally, "of the mountains," and also the name of a prominent clan), and the other is known as gadoʔa, in reference to a gnarled juniper tree, still standing, near which the ancestors of the present inhabitants laid out farms.

On the west side of the Creek, roughly opposite dzɨłtadn and gadoʔa, sections are not so clearly defined. The people here are of mixed ancestry, so to speak, some having been members of the Carizzo band, and others reckoning back to local groups originally located in the Cibecue and White Springs regions. The most common term for this portion of Cibecue is tlukadɨgaidn, a clan name which is also extended to all Apaches living in the present community of Carizzo.

The smallest and northernmost section, located on an elevated flat overlooking Cibecue valley is called haitɨn ("on top"). This is a place name and marks the spot where the present dwellers made their camps after moving to Cibecue from the area around White Springs, some 15 miles to the north.

Apaches in Cibecue will sometimes speak of certain clans as being associated with certain sections. Historically this was probably true, but recently gathered census data indicates that with three or four exceptions the associations are actually quite weak. The majority of clans are well represented in more than one section, and a few are represented in all. In short, section boundaries are difficult to define in terms of clan kinship, and Apaches themselves get confused when asked to do so. Sections are best thought of as territorial divisions of a rather vestigial character whose inhabitants claim ancestry to local groups now defunct.

The minimal residential unit in Cibecue is the gową. As used by the Apache, this term refers to both the occupants and the location of a single dwelling or, as is more apt to be the case, several dwellings built within a few feet of each other. Although the majority of gową are occupied by a married couple and their unmarried children, it should be emphasized that gową composition is highly variable. This is of minor consequence to the Apache, however, who classifies all gową as equivalent, regardless of differences in internal structure. What matters to the Indian is that the individuals living in a gową, including those residing there temporarily, are almost certainly related by very close ties of kinship and, as a consequence, if asked to join in some enterprise will accept or decline as a unit.

J. B. is an Apache about fifty years old who, together with his wife and five children, occupies a gową in the dzⅰɫtadn section of Cibecue. It is located near a grove of cottonwood trees about 30 yards from Cibecue Creek. J. B., his wife, and their infant son live in a small one-room house. The other four children sleep in a wickiup nearby. In the winter, when it gets very cold, the children move in with their parents. Close to the wickiup there is a shade, or ramada, a rectangular structure with walls made of brush. During the summer, the shade is a center of activity. Here the children play, J. B.'s wife prepares the family's food, and visitors are entertained.

J. B. himself was born into another gową, located several miles to the south of where he lives now. He recalls:

When I got married, I moved to where my wife was living with her parents. We stayed there for about one year but it was too crowded. Then my wife's mother said we should live where my wife's sister used to live (a gową about 75 yards away). So we came over to where we are living now. There was already this house here, but we had to build a wickiup and a shade. So we did. . . .

After we came to this place I used to get homesick for where my own people lived down the creek. I used to go down there a lot, just to visit my relatives. Then one time my wife got mad at me. She said: "Why do you go away from here all the time? Don't you like it here? This is where you live now and you should stay here." Pretty soon my wife had a baby and I think she felt better about me after that. So I didn't go away so much—just stayed around this place.

Now I am used to living up here. It's a pretty good place and my children like it. Now I am like one of these people around here and I only go back (home) when someone dies or they sing for someone who is sick. People come here to find me now because they know I live here and have lived here a long time.

There are approximately 130 gową sites in Cibecue, but at least fifteen are presently vacant. Of those which are occupied seventy-four are made up of large nuclear families; seventeen of a widowed or divorced parent and his or her unmarried children; five of a set of grandparents and an unmarried granddaughter with or without offspring; three of married couples without children; and two of a single grandparent and his or her unmarried children. Six gową are occupied by widowed individuals living alone. This summary gives a somewhat illusory impression of tidiness in gową structure, for it frequently happens that besides the individuals who regularly reside in a camp one or more other persons are present. In many cases, these are unmarried children by former marriages or close relatives, either divorced or widowed, who were asked to visit at some time in the past and were persuaded to remain.

For example, in 1961 the wife of H. B., J. B.'s older brother, died of pneumonia. Shortly thereafter, H. B. started to live with J. B.

After they buried his wife, my brother tried to stay where he had been living with that woman. He tried to sleep there at night but he couldn't fall asleep. One time he heard something—like his wife calling to him—and got scared. After that, he didn't want to stay there anymore, so he started sleeping down here, sometimes in the shade. He was pretty old and had no money, so my wife gave him food because I didn't think anybody would cook for him.

He was pretty old but even so he helped me out. He shoed my horses and helped me get firewood. One time he got some money and gave $20.00 to my wife. He used to get drunk but he never got mean or angry, so we didn't make him go.

My brother stayed around here for maybe three years. Then my sister's husband died, so he went to her camp, down there by the Mission School. Now she is the one who cooks for him.

He is still down there, but I think he is getting blind. He doesn't come back anymore. . . . Yes, he will stay there from now on.

Persons living in the same gową cooperate closely. While the wife (mother) and her adolescent daughters tend to household chores, the husband (father) works at a job or, as the case may be, derives a small income from government checks. For the most part, money stays within the family where it is used to purchase essentials like food and clothing, to make payments at the trading post and, not infrequently, to acquire liberal quantities of beer and wine. The increasing (but by no means complete) economic self-sufficiency of the individual gową is viewed with disapproval by older Apaches who criticize job-holders for not being more generous with their wages. Said one old man:

When I was growing up I lived at Oak Creek and there were about ten gową down there. All those gową shared with each other. If some of those people had no food they could get it from another gową.

One time in the winter the men went hunting. But they had bad luck and didn't kill any deer. The next day it was the same way. The same again, the day after that. Then all those men went out again. All except one had bad luck. The man who had good luck killed four deer—all at the same place. It took him all day to butcher them. That night, he took the meat from three deer and went around with it to all those other *gową*. He gave meat to the people who were hungry. Some were not his relatives, but he gave it to them anyway because he knew they were hungry. . . .

Today some of these *gową* in Cibecue have money. Some of them own lots of cattle and have good jobs. But they keep their money and don't share it. If they gave it away, they say, their babies would starve, but they could spare some of it. I know that.

Despite its emerging primacy as an economic unit, and for all its internal solidarity, the individual *gową* is by no means an autonomous social unit. Its affairs, and indeed to a limited extent its continued welfare, are intimately bound up with several other *gową*, specifically those which comprise what the Apache labels a *gota* or, following Goodwin, a "family cluster."

The term *gota* refers to a group of spatially localized *gową* each of which has at least one member, generally an adult married female, who is related by ties of matrilineal kinship to persons living in all the others. Today, as in pre-reservation times, a single *gota* may contain as many as eight *gową* and, owing to the continued preference for matrilocal residence, usually takes the form of a matrilocal extended family.

Although the *gota* no longer provides the organizational framework for economic activities such as food-gathering, the loss of this function has in no obvious way damaged its internal cohesiveness. The women whose lineage consti-tutes the core of the *gota* and from whose clan the *gota* derives its name, are together almost constantly—washing clothes, grinding corn, collecting firewood, cooking, and helping tend each other's children. It is common for the Apache to liken the women of a *gota* to the trunk of a tree, their children to its branches, and their husbands to its leaves. "The leaves drop off," it is said, "but the branches and the trunk never break."

Men who marry into a *gota* are still called upon to show respect in the presence of their parents-in-law and to help them in whatever way possible. The latter are apt to point out that the most expedient kind of aid would be gifts of money, but most sons-in-law, together with their wives, recognize that such gen-erosity could threaten the survival of their own *gową*. Occasionally a man will give his wife's parents a few dollars, but for the most part he helps them by performing heavy physical tasks. Nonetheless it is a frequent complaint that sons-in-law today think only of themselves and have forgotten how to "carry baskets" in the proper time-honored fashion.

Thinking back to the time when he was first married, J. B. says:

We lived close by to my wife's parents then. I knew they were watching me, to see how I would take care of my new wife. Before I went there, my father said: "Act good and don't drink because your wife's relatives will be watching to see if you do bad things." So I stayed there. I only went away to visit my relatives. I couldn't drink much, even when I wanted. Most of the time I just stayed there with my wife.

After about two months, I got a job working here in Cibecue. I got pretty good money that time, so I gave some to my wife and held on to some. Pretty soon, I had enough to buy two horses. So I did. That same day, my wife's parents heard about it and I guess they got angry. They said to my wife: "Why does your husband use his money on himself? Why doesn't he give it to you? We are poor people and you should ask him to give some of that money to us." My wife didn't get angry at me. She just told me what her parents had said. I started to worry about it, but for a long time I didn't do anything.

Then we moved to where we live now and, just before we did, I gave my father-in-law one of those horses I had bought with that money. I guess he liked that. He rides that horse now, and my wife's parents never said anything again to my wife about me.

For all the strains and tensions that may be involved in living with his wife's parents, a man who provides well for his family and who shows himself to be of even temper is quickly welcomed into the *gota*. If he makes friends easily, and especially if he is adept at persuading other people to work for him, his position in the *gota* becomes more secure, and his opinions are sought on matters of importance. Eventually his father-in-law will come to him and say: "My son-in-law, I have been looking out for the people in these camps for many years. But now I am getting old. Your children are part of these people now. I think you should watch out for our camps."

As noted earlier, the local group ceased to exist as a spatially distinct unit when the various Western Apache bands took leave of their original territories and settled permanently near trading posts and government schools. This shift had two major effects: residential isolation ceased to be a critical factor in the organization of social life; and the clan system assumed greater importance than ever before (Kaut 1957:72). In Cibecue, as in other settlements, clan members whose local groups had been separated by wide distances found themselves in daily contact, with the result that concerted action as a group became decidedly easier than in pre-reservation times. Also, persons belonging to unrelated clans were drawn into closer proximity, and clan differences were accentuated to an unprecedented degree.

As used by the Apache living in Cibecue the term *hatiʔi* may refer either to a single clan or, more specifically, to those representatives of a clan who reside together in the same settlement. Bilingual Apaches use the word "branch" to distinguish the latter sense of *hatiʔi* from the former, which is most often translated as "line."

The "branches" of twenty-one clans are located in Cibecue, but two of these are represented by single individuals only (both old men), and within a few years the number of clans will almost certainly be reduced to nineteen. The "branches" vary in size. Some, like the *desčidn* and the *iyaʔaiye*, have well over one hundred members while others, like the *tiskʔadn* and *bιzάhά*, contain less than twenty.

On the basis of phratry relationships the twenty-one clans may be grouped into three segments, recognized but unnamed by the Apache, whose composition is shown in Table 3. These segments, like the "branches" that comprise them, are not residential kin groups, and representatives of at least two reside in each of Cibecue's six major sections. Some "branches" have nonhereditary chiefs (*hatiʔi nantan*), older men whose advice is sought on matters of importance to the entire group, such as impending marriages, ceremonial plans, and sending children to school off the reservation.

Members of the same clan "branch" regularly turn to each other in times of crisis and make a point of exchanging small favors whenever possible. Work groups—such as those required for the construction of a new wickiup or ramada— are usually composed of persons related by clan. When a drinking party is held clan members are the first to hear about it and, upon arrival, can expect to be given the most generous portions of whatever beverage is being consumed. Major items of material culture, and particularly rifles, saddles, and pick-up trucks, are readily loaned to clan members who can be relied on to return them in good condition. Nowhere is the unity of the clan "branch" so evident as in the long and costly preparations which precede major ceremonials, notably the girls' puberty rite. Work is begun fully two months in advance, and throughout the preliminaries clan relatives of the pubescent girl contribute heavily, both with substantial gifts of money and long hours of physical labor. The distinction made between an entire clan ("line") and its residentially localized "branches" is significant, for although clan membership still serves to establish meaningful relationships be- tween individuals in different settlements, the Apache openly admits that his

TABLE 3
CLANS REPRESENTED IN CIBECUE, GROUPED ACCORDING TO
PHRATRY AFFILIATION

Phratry Number 1
  iyaʔaiye (?)
  tenadoljage (?)
  tuʔagaidn ("white water people")
  tseʔdesgaidn ("horizontal white rock people")
  kiyaʔan ("below a house people")
  saidιgaidn ("lines of white sand joining people")
  dzιltadn ("foot of the mountain people")
  tlukadιgaidn ("row of white canes people")
  ndιčidntʔidn ("two rows of yellow pine joining people")
  čιlčosιkʔadn ("Gambel's oak standing people")

Phratry Number 2
  dušdoę ("flies in soup people")
  beilson (?)
  bιzahą ("*bιzahą* people"); named after farm site near Whiteriver
  tsečιsčιne ("rocks jutting out people")
  daʔιskan ("flat top people")
  nasołčιn ("manzanita extending up people")

Phratry Number 3
  saikine ("Papago/Pima people")
  desčidn ("horizontal red people")
  gadoʔan ("juniper standing alone people")
  tiskʔadn ("cottonwood standing people")
  kιsdesčinaditιn ("trail through horizontal red alders people")

closest ties and most demanding obligations are with clan kin who live nearby. This points up an important feature of contemporary Western Apache social organization: whereas the solidarity of "branches" is strong, the ties which bind disparate branches together are breaking down.

The following incident, described by an informant who was involved in it, serves as an illustration.

One time my brother wanted to have *nai?es* (girls' puberty ceremonial) for his daughter. He needed help for that, so he went around to the people here who are *bɩzahɑ* (his clan). He said: "I want you to help me set up a dance for my daughter. Help me if you can—that way the dance will be a good one." Those people all listened to him and most of them promised him something. But still my brother didn't have enough.

Then he went to Whiteriver where there are lots of *bɩzahɑ*. He went to many camps and said what he had said before. "You people, can you help me put up a dance for my daughter. I want it to be a good one so help me any way you can." But over there they didn't want to do it. Only my brother's cousin gave him something. My brother was in Whiteriver two days. Those were his relatives he went to, but they said they couldn't help. So he just stopped going around and came back here. After that he was sad because he didn't think he would have a dance for his daughter.

Similarly, there have been signs of instability in phratry structure. Members of the same clan still do not marry, but within the past thirteen years two marriages have taken place in Cibecue between persons whose clans were "closely related." Though both were roundly denounced, it is clear nevertheless that the exogamous proscriptions which once applied to all clans within a clan section are starting to weaken. That they have remained in force this long is noteworthy because evidence of their violation on the San Carlos Reservation was recorded as early as 1935 when Goodwin (1935:60) wrote: "Today . . . the clan system remains only partially intact . . . marriage between related clans is sometimes allowed."

Of greater significance to the individual Apache is the fact that phratry obligations have become increasingly less viable. As one man said: "It used to be that you could count on those people all the time because they were related to you, but lots of them don't act like brothers anymore." Said another: "People in your own line (clan) are good to go to for help, but nowadays you can't count on your other lines (related clans)."

To sum up: since the establishment of reservations in the 1870s, traditional Western Apache social organization has undergone several profound alterations. Primary among these has been the formation of settlements and the concomitant disappearance of bands and local groups. The family cluster, or *gota*, has been stripped of its earlier economic functions which have devolved largely upon the individual nuclear household, or *gowɑ*. Clan "branches" continue to function as unified social groups, but connections between "branches" in different settlements have lost much of their earlier importance. Finally, restrictions prohibiting the marriage of persons in related clans are breaking down, and phratry membership no longer entails the observance of a multiplicity of reciprocal obligations.

Social Structure

Despite the recent changes in social organization, Western Apache kinship terminology has remained surprisingly stable. With one or two exceptions, the terms continue to be used in a manner similar to that described by Goodwin.

Older Apaches are apt to claim that members of the younger generations are not as proficient in matters of kinship as they should be, but my experience indicates that this is true only in the sense that young people are not altogether certain who their relatives in other settlements are. They do not regard this as a serious problem, however, and if they did, as one informant pointed out, it could be easily remedied. Said he: "If I had to find out who my relatives are in White-river or some place like that, I'd just ask my mother or my mother's sister."

Before moving on to a discussion of present-day kinship behavior, note should be taken of a set of terms (not reported by Goodwin) which categorize persons on the basis of clan affiliation. These terms are important for several reasons. First, they are used frequently. Second, they serve to classify persons at a higher level of generality—and with greater simplicity—than conventional kinship terms. And third, as we shall see later on, they embody distinctions that figure predominantly in the identification of witch suspects.

The term *ki* applies to all persons who belong to clans related to one's own; that is, all members of Ego's phratry except those in his own clan. The latter, Ego's clan relatives, are labeled *ki ąthanıgo*. All individuals not subsumed under these two categories are called *dohwakida*. There are three types of *dohwakida*: *banestį*—persons belonging to the clan of Ego's father; *šaʔadni*—persons belonging to the clan of Ego's spouse; and finally *dohandago*—persons who are *dohwakida*, but who belong neither to Ego's father's clan nor to that of his spouse (see Figure 6).

The basic features of kinship behavior remain much as Goodwin described them, and the brevity of what follows is dictated by a wish to avoid repetition. The Western Apache's strongest ties are with those of his *ki ąthanıgo* who comprise his own lineage and clan "branch." Restraint typifies interaction with older members of this group (especially maternal grandparents) and also with siblings and parallel cousins of the opposite sex. Institutionalized joking between both sets of cross-cousin, regardless of sex, persists in undiluted form.

The most conspicuous deviation from the pattern described by Goodwin has to do with the loss of instrumental authority by the mother's brother. This, as I have argued elsewhere (Basso, n.d.), is directly related to the emergence of the nuclear household as a semi-independent economic unit and, more specifically, to the concomitant assumption of increased authority by Ego's father. Although the mother's brother no longer plays the major part he once did in the upbringing of his sister's son, his role as confidant and counselor continues. A young Apache in need of advice is still apt to seek out his mother's brother rather than his father, and he explains this by saying that the former is more sympathetic and less likely to dismiss the matter, however minor, as inconsequential.

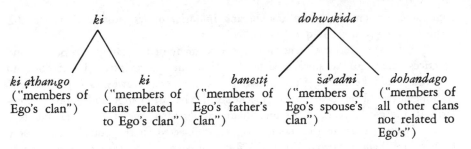

ki			*dohwakida*	
ki ałhan₁go ("members of Ego's clan")	*ki* ("members of clans related to Ego's clan")	*banestị* ("members of Ego's father's clan")	*ša'adni* ("members of Ego's spouse's clan")	*dohandago* ("members of all other clans not related to Ego's")

Figure 6. Classifications of persons on basis of clan and phratry affiliations.

The frequently voiced characterization of *banestị* as "too busy to bother with you" points up the tangential involvement of paternal kin in the Apache's daily affairs. Obligations between Ego and his father's relatives are weak, and it is generally the case that they approach each other for aid only when other resources have been exhausted.

Although an Apache's *ša'adni* are spoken of as "people who must be worked for," it is noteworthy that this aspect of affinal relationships become less and less pronounced as a son-in-law consolidates his position in his wife's *gota*. Mother-in-law avoidance is still practiced, and familiarities of any sort between Ego and his unmarried sisters-in-law are frowned upon. However, this is not the case with brothers-in-law, who are free to joke with one another and, of all *ša'adni*, are said to be the "easiest to know."

Religion

Of all the settlements on the Fort Apache Reservation, Cibecue is regarded as the most conservative. Apaches living there, together with those from other settlements, say it has "a long ride ahead" (that is, modernization is years away), and in support of this opinion usually offer one or more of the following reasons:

1. Until recently, the majority of Cibecue's inhabitants lived in traditional grass wickiups. Many still do.

2. Cibecue has more medicine men presently active than any other settlement. (There are four medicine men in Cibecue, at least two more than in any of the eight other settlements.)

3. More ceremonials are held in Cibecue than anywhere else. (For example, between June 1 and September 30, 1965, forty-one ceremonials were performed. Over the same period of time, Whiteriver, with a substantially larger population, was second with twenty-nine.)

4. At ceremonials, rodeos, and other social events, it is commonly said that people from Cibecue prefer to keep to themselves, being reluctant to mix with Apaches from other settlements.

There is evidence to indicate that in most basic respects Cibecue's social organization and social structure are paralleled elsewhere, especially in Carizzo and East Fork. According to Apaches, what distinguishes Cibecue most obviously from other settlements is the amount and intensity of its ritual activity. In this respect, they say it is unique.

Since we will have occasion to describe many of the categories, beliefs, and practices central to Western Apache "religion" in the chapters that follow, no purpose would be served by summarizing them here. However, a few general comments should be made about Cibecue's resistance to change and, more particularly, to the recalcitrance of its inhabitants to abandon traditional ceremonialism.

Situated high in the mountains, and connected to the outside world only by horse trails and a narrow dirt road, Cibecue was for a long time the most remote settlement on the Fort Apache Reservation. Unlike the communities of Cedar Creek, Canyon Day, and Whiteriver—which are located just off Arizona Highway 60—it was never readily accessible to outsiders and up until recently, when work was begun to widen and pave the road, it had experienced a minimum of contact with bearers of Western culture. Geographical isolation has no doubt contributed significantly to Cibecue's conservatism, but in the minds of the people who live there, other, less obvious factors account for the persistence of native ritual.

Primary among these is the widespread conviction that because of the skill of its resident medicine men, ceremonials are more apt to be effective in Cibecue than elsewhere. The people say this has always been true, but it was dramatically demonstrated once again in 1942 when a war dance was held for seven young Apaches about to join U.S. combat forces overseas. Each man was blessed with "Bat Power" (ǰapane biyiɁ), thus enabling him to dodge bullets with the same ease as a bat avoids obstacles in the dark. The power worked impressively, for although two of the soldiers were seriously wounded all seven returned home alive.

There was also the case of F. N., a Cibecue woman in her late fifties, who in 1958 was informed by physicians that she had a terminal case of tuberculosis. Faced with the unhappy prospect of dying alone in the unfamiliar atmosphere of a hospital, F. N. requested that she be allowed to return home to Cibecue. Immediately upon her arrival, her husband made arrangements for a gan ceremonial, the most potent of all Western Apache curing rituals. It spanned four nights. Midway through the first, F. N., who had come back to Cibecue on a stretcher, sat up and sipped some broth. During the second night, she requested solid food. Her condition did not improve on the third night, but on the fourth she stood up and took a few tentative steps. Today she is still very ill but alive nevertheless.

These events, and others equally dramatic, have been recounted so often that they have come to comprise a sort of informal mythology which functions to reinforce and sustain belief in the effectiveness of ceremonials and the skill of the men who conduct them.

It should be emphasized that by Apache standards the medicine men in Cibecue are a select group. Two are held in especially high esteem because they were trained by Willie Neal, probably the most widely renowned medicine man to appear among the Western Apache since the turn of the century. Willie Neal died recently in a rest home in Phoenix, but his accomplishments have not been forgotten. Among other things, he is credited with having predicted long before automobiles and pick-up trucks made their appearance on Fort Apache that "iron objects with eyes that see in the night" would one day be commonplace. Primarily, however, he was known as a man whose knowledge of curing ritual was unsurpassed. Those of his disciples presently living in Cibecue—medicine men who have achieved notable success in their own right—regularly cite their association with Willie Neal as proof of their expertise and the validity of their ceremonials. For the majority of Apaches no further proof is needed.

Although Western Apache ritual is decidely cure-oriented, it does not conflict directly with the medical facilities provided by the hospital at Whiteriver. The Apache recognize that many symptoms respond quickly to Western medicine and, in many cases, show little reluctance in bringing them to the attention of the white physicians. But they also believe that in certain critical areas—such as the diagnosis of disease *causes* and the bestowal of protection against the recurrence of causes—the white doctor is woefully deficient. These are matters which require special knowledge, medicine men, and ceremonials. As long as this attitude persists, ceremonialism is likely to flourish, for native ritual provides answers, available from no other source, to questions that are of paramount importance to the Apache's physical and psychological welfare.

3

The Realm of Power

ONE DAY in July, an Apache boy dismounted from his horse in front of his wickiup and drank from a pail of water that his mother had drawn a few hours before from Cibecue Creek. He went inside the wickiup, lay down, and fell asleep. He was awakened an hour or so later by severe abdominal cramps. The pains persisted and in the evening, when his mother noticed that he seemed pale, he informed her that he was sick.

"Eat," said his mother, "and your paining may leave you alone." The boy had some soup and a tortilla, but afterwards he felt no better. "You should sleep," his mother said, "and your stomach paining may have left you alone in the morning." The boy was able to sleep a little, but when the sun rose he felt worse than before. "I don't know why you are sick," said his mother. "Yesterday you felt good and now your stomach is eating at itself. I think we should find out why it is this way. I have thought about it and think a medicine man can find out for you."

That night a medicine man came to the sick boy's camp, and after questioning the lad about his recent activities, sang twelve Bear songs. When he had finished, he announced that he had learned why the boy was ill. "You drank water that a bear bathed in. Your mother didn't know it when she got that water, but it was the same a bear swam in. Now that bear is making your stomach eat at itself. You are sick from the power of the bear."

* * *

Shortly before midnight, an elderly Apache woman lay down to sleep. Across the wickiup from her bed, on a small table near the door, she had left a few dishes from the evening meal and a lighted kerosene lantern. The woman was awakened from her sleep by a loud noise. She looked to see what it was and saw, standing less than a yard away, one of her maternal aunts, a woman who had died over twenty years ago.

I was sure scared when I saw that ghost. I wanted to know why that woman came back. So I said to her: "My aunt, my aunt, what do you want from me?"

34

But she didn't say anything. So I said it again to her: "Auntie, what do you come back to do?" But she didn't answer again. Then that ghost sat down at the table, and I could see her face from the light in that lantern. Then she started to rattle those dishes, make lots of noise. I didn't say anything after that. I was too scared. Then, when I didn't say anything, that ghost just went outside. I waited for a long time and didn't hear anything. When I got up, my nose sure start to bleeding—all over my dress and arms. Then I knew that ghost came back to hurt me.

The next morning, the Apache woman visited her sister and explained in detail what had happened. The sister said: "Go to a medicine man, and he will pray for you. If you don't, that ghost will come back and make you sick again. The medicine man can make it stay away."

* * *

It was August, 1962, and preparations were in progress for a puberty ceremonial. A dance-ground had been cleared at a site 2 miles north of Cibecue, and relatives of the girl for whom the ceremonial was being given had set up camps nearby. The girl herself was seated on the ground next to her maternal grandmother who was making tortillas. The old woman spoke:

My maternal grandchild, it is good these people are having that dance for you. It will make you strong. Do just what that medicine man tells you.
When I was a girl I had a dance like that, and I am still strong. I have grey hair and my ears plug up, but my body is still strong. These people around here say it: that old woman may be old, but she never gets lazy. Works hard all the time. My legs are strong, and I can still walk long ways. My eyes see the sun in the morning. Some old people are running down but I keep pretty strong. That dance I had made it that way for me. That is why it is good for you to have it. That way it can be the same for you. So when the medicine man works with his power from Changing Woman (an important figure in Western Apache mythology), do just what he says. If you don't do it that way, you may get sick when you are old and have a short life.

* * *

One afternoon a few summers ago an Apache woman left her camp on Cibecue Creek and, together with her two youngest children, started to walk to the nearest trading post. The day was hot and humid, without breeze, and the woman noticed a heavy bank of clouds in the sky to the north. "It will rain in the late day," she said to one of the children.

Outside the trading post, the woman met her maternal parallel cousin and together they sat down to talk. They had not seen each other for several weeks and there was much to discuss—a new marriage, a forthcoming curing ceremonial, the high prices at the trading post, and a fight the night before during which a man had been seriously injured. An hour or so later, when the women had run out of things to say, they parted company, and the one who had come with her children entered the trading post. She was in a hurry now because the clouds in the north had moved closer.

Inside the trading post it was quiet, and the first drops of rain were clearly audible as they smacked against the roof. Within moments it was raining heavily. Suddenly there was a sharp clap of thunder and, right behind it, lightning. The storm grew in intensity and continued unabated for about ten minutes. Then, abruptly, it stopped.

The woman bought a few groceries and hurried home. There she saw that a large cottonwood tree, no more than 20 yards from her wickiup, had been struck by lightning. Small pieces of wood lay scattered on the ground, and the trunk of the tree, now badly shattered, was smoking.

The woman put down her groceries and walked down the creek to the camp of an experienced medicine man. "Something bad has happened at my camp," she said to him. "Lightning has come too close to it. I want you to sing for that camp so no one will get sick and that lightning won't come so close again."

That night the medicine man went to the woman's camp and conducted a "lightning ceremony." Shortly before it ended, he announced: "I think everything will be all right. That lightning will stay away now and nobody living here will get sick."

Power and Its Uses

The distinction made by Westerners between things "natural" and "supernatural" has no exact equivalent in the culture of the Western Apache. For example, powers, mythological figures, and ghosts are construed by Apaches as existing on roughly the same par with such things as the sun, rain, wind, and even certain kinds of mineral; they are every bit as tangible and every bit as "real." Although these entities have access to supra-terrestrial regions denied to man, they often appear in his midst and regularly get involved in his affairs. At such times they may be addressed like human beings, and it is expected that in one way or another they will respond. They are thought to behave according to rules similar to those influencing the actions of men, and it is on this assumption that Apaches interact with them. In short, they are not conceptualized as belonging to an order of phenomena radically opposed to that which makes up the natural world. Nor are they considered to operate independently of the immediate surroundings in which man finds himself and his society. They are integral components of these surroundings, and they are approached and dealt with accordingly.

At a very general level, the Western Apache partition their universe into three classes of phenomena. One of these, labeled *hinda*, refers to things that are capable of generating and sustaining their own locomotive movement, and includes man, quadrupeds, birds, reptiles, amphibians, fish, insects, all flora, and a few types of machines such as automobiles, tractors, bulldozers, and road-graders. A second category, *destą*, denotes objects that are either immobile or depend for movement upon the intervention of outside forces; it encompasses all topographical features and every item of material culture except for motorized vehicles and those additional few that are *godiyo*. This, the third major category, refers to things that are "holy" and includes ceremonials, certain items of ritual paraphernalia, celestial bodies, wind, rain, thunder, lightning, myths, mythological beings, ghosts and, perhaps most important, the several varieties of *diyıʔ*, which we shall gloss here simply as "power." Beyond the fact that it possesses the attribute of "holiness," the concept of power resists rigorous definition. Apaches are quite specific about what power does and which things possess it, but they have difficulty explaining just what power is. Furthermore, they seem convinced that any attempt to do so will prove unsatisfactory. On one occasion, toward the end of a lengthy conversation which had been conducted in Apache, my informant, a bilingual, switched abruptly into English and said: "You can't talk about *diyi*ʔ like other things. You can't hold it with words. So don't try on it anymore."

Elsewhere, I have described power as follows:

> The term *diyi*ʔ refers to one or all of a set of abstract and invisible forces which are said to derive from certain classes of animals, plants, minerals, meteorological phenomena, and mythological figures within the Western Apache universe. Any of the various powers may be 'acquired' by man . . . and used for a variety of purposes (Basso 1966:150).

For the moment, let us think of power simply as a critical attribute of any class of objects that is said to possess it. As can be seen from the following list, these classes provide the criteria according to which powers are categorized and distinguished from one another.

*tu biyi*ʔ ("Water Power")

*kɔbiyi*ʔ ("Fire Power")

*edidi biyi*ʔ ("Thunder Power")

*nagołti biyi*ʔ ("Rain Power")

*iłti biyi*ʔ ("Lightning Power")

*iłči biyi*ʔ ("Wind Power")

*klegonaʔai biyi*ʔ ("Moon Power")

*čonaʔai biyi*ʔ ("Sun Power")

*gan biyi*ʔ ("*Gan* Power"). The *gan* are a set of male dieties who, in the context of a ceremonial bearing their name (*gan gojitał*), manifest themselves in the form of masked dancers.

*istsənadlęžę biyi*ʔ ("Changing Woman, her power"). The "power" of *istsənadlęžę*, a female mythological figure, which is invoked during the girls' puberty ceremonial.

*izeʔbiyi*ʔ ("Root Power"). This refers specifically to the root of the manzanita (*nos*) which is used for a variety of medicinal purposes.

*šəš biyi*ʔ ("Bear Power")

*itsa biyi*ʔ ("Eagle Power")

*kliš tsetsuk biyi*ʔ ("Snake Power")

*łi biyi*ʔ ("Horse Power")

*makəši biyi*ʔ ("Cattle Power")

*ndučo biyi*ʔ ("Mountain Lion Power")

*jage biyi*ʔ ("Prong-horn Antelope Power")

*bi biyi*ʔ ("Black-tailed or Mule Deer Power")

*tseʔe biyi*ʔ ("White-tailed Deer Power")

*binalde biyi*ʔ ("Elk Power")

*našo biyi*ʔ ("Lizard Power")

nadn²ai biyɩ² ("Pole Power")
bɔse biyɩ² ("Hoop Power")
ĵapane biyɩ² ("Bat Power")
mba biyɩ² ("Wolf Power")
mbatsose biyɩ² ("Coyote Power")
təži biyɩ² ("Wild Turkey Power")

According to the Apache, there is an inexhaustible supply of each power in the universe. A small percentage of it can be acquired by man and brought under his control, but the remainder stays free, so to speak, to act on its own. This latter portion does not possess moral sanctity, nor is it considered by Apaches to be inherently benevolent. To the contrary, if a power is offended by what it considers disrespectful behavior it is capable of causing extreme hardship.

Theoretically, powers are available to everyone, but many Apaches—the large majority in fact—do not possess them. One reason for this is that acquiring a power or, in Apache terms, "getting to own it," requires an investment of time, energy, and money that most people cannot afford. Then, too, there is the consideration that a power can impose burdensome responsibilities and, not infrequently, incite fear and jealousy in other people. Apaches believe that a power is a valuable and useful thing to have, that it can make life easier, more rewarding, and even prolong it. But while admitting that persons without a power are at a disadvantage, they also say that acquiring one may lead to troubles that might otherwise be avoided.

The fact that many Apaches do not possess power should not lead us to think that it plays an insignificant part in their lives. To the contrary, owing to the fact that power is inextricably bound up with experiences familiar to everyone—sickness, death, bad luck, strained social relations—it is something that must be confronted and reckoned with continually.

A sharp distinction is made between Apaches who possess a power (*diyɩn*), and those who do not. The former include medicine men, or shamans, who manipulate their power on behalf of others, primarily to diagnose and cure sickness. But the *diyɩn* category also includes individuals who direct their powers to more personal (and less conspicuous) ends, such as discovering the whereabouts of lost objects, heightening the chances of success in hunting, and predicting future events.

The uses to which a power can be put are varied but not unlimited, and each man must learn through trial and error what his is capable of doing. If a power fails at one type of activity, its owner takes careful note and refrains from using it for that purpose again. Conversely, if the power succeeds at some other task, its owner gains confidence and is encouraged to call for a repeat performance. In this way, through protracted experimentation, the Apache discovers what his power can accomplish. Individuals who have owned a power for many years know exactly what to expect from it; persons who have only recently acquired a power are less certain.

It should be clearly understood that two men, each with the same type of power, may use it in different ways. For one man "Black-tailed Deer Power" may be helpful in hunting but not in gambling. For another man the situation may be completely reversed. In short, what matters is not so much the type of power involved as what experience has shown its owner it can do best and most often.

Some of the uses, other than curing, to which Apaches put their powers are described below:

> On horses, mostly. Sometimes they get wild and don't want to let you ride them. I use it then, to make them gentle. In the morning, sometimes, I can't find my horses. They wander off. It tells me where they are and I can go then to find them.

> The one I know, I use it for lots of things. Deer hunting, sometimes. It can tell me when to go and take me to a place where it's easy to kill one. Easy places, where it isn't hard to pack the meat out.

> It's gone now, but I had it one time. It just watched out for me mostly. Once, when they played *še* (a native gambling game) over at Oak Creek, I was sure far behind. Then I went away from where they were playing and prayed to it. When I came back I started to win. My power made it that way.

> I tell it to keep my kids from getting sick. Before I got it, our first baby died. Just overnight. Then I got it. We had six children and they don't get sick. It knows what I want it to do is good, so it does it.

> That time, my boy went away to boarding school. I sure was lonely for that boy. I cry for him. My power, I told it just to watch out for my son when he was away from home. Then I got a letter from him, and he said he had a dream about me and where I live. Right here. After that, I didn't worry so much for that boy. My power, it was watching out for him.

Besides aiding its owner in the performance of specific tasks, a power acts in a more generalized capacity, that of providing protection against misfortune. Under normal circumstances, this is not a service which an Apache feels compelled to request. He simply assumes that if he behaves towards his power in the appropriate fashion, taking care at all times not to offend it, the bestowal of protection will follow as a matter of course. However, in the event that amicable relations with the power are upset, it may decide to withdraw its protection, thereby exposing its owner to serious danger.

Apaches say that the surest way to maintain effective contact with a power is to accord it the same courtesies customarily extended to human beings. For example, instructions given by a power, however onerous, should be carried out without complaint or suppressed ill feeling. When making requests, the power should be addressed politely and spoken to in a low, unhurried key; it should never be "bossed around." Having rendered a service, it should be given tangible payment, either with prayers of thanks, or by singing several of the chants associated with it. In short, viable and productive interaction with a power, like viable and productive interaction with other people, requires conscious effort and attention. It cannot be taken for granted. Failure to observe the appropriate social forms can engender hostility and this, in turn, can lead to termination of the relationship.

When an Apache loses his power, he feels despondent, lonely, and afraid.

Not only has he been divested of a barrier against misfortune, but the possibility exists that the power, angry at him and knowing that he lacks protection, will try to seek revenge by inflicting sickness. Attempts are sometimes made to recover lost powers, but there is general agreement that the chances of success are slim. Once the bond between a power and its owner has been broken, it is virtually irreparable.

I have recorded only six cases of powers deserting their owners. In three of these, the power departed because it was displeased at having been mistreated. In the other three it was unhappy because its owner had advanced in years to the points where he was "too weak" to use it to maximum advantage.

The Apache emphasize that a correlation exists between the effectiveness of a power and the physical condition of its owner. More specifically, a power is most responsive when its owner is in the prime of life or, in Apache terms, when he has reached the age-stage *mbaiyən*. Used in reference to both men and women, this term is first applied when an individual is between the ages of thirty to thirty-six years. It remains in effect until the point of sexual inactivity is reached, at which time it is supplanted by *hastin* (for males) and *san* (for females). The Apache say that when a man becomes *hastin* his ability to manipulate a power starts to weaken. This is a slow process though, and many people retain their power for as long as they live. In a few cases, however, the power gets restless and wishes to transfer itself to someone more vigorous. The owner is sorry to see it go but knows there is nothing he can do to stop it. He thanks the power for the help that it has given and wishes it well. The partnership is then dissolved.

The Acquisition of a Power

An Apache may acquire a power in either one of two ways. In the first, called *diyi? šaniya* ("power finds you"), a power, acting on its own, selects some individual to be its owner. In the second, called *diyi? baniya* ("you find power"), the situation is reversed: a would-be owner selects a power. For the Apache, this distinction has considerable importance.

Persons who have been sought out by a power are considered especially worthy and qualified. After all, the reasoning goes, they did not have to find a power; it came to them. On the other hand, individuals who have not been approached lack this sign of tacit approval, with the result that the validity of their claim to a power may be questioned. This is not invariably so, however, and there are several instances where persons in the latter category have achieved wide renown. Nevertheless, it is a significant fact that all of the medicine men in Cibecue acquired a power because it, not they, took the initiative.

POWER FINDS YOU. Initial contact between a power and the person it chooses to be its owner can take several forms. That to which greatest value is attached begins with the appearance in a dream of a power-source (a black-tailed deer, for example), which notifies the dreamer that its power ("Black-tailed Deer Power") is available for acquisition. In most cases this message is accompanied by instructions to learn the chants and prayers associated with the power, for without these it cannot be properly manipulated or controlled.

Apaches to whom powers have been offered in dreams recall the experience as intense and unforgettable.

> Long ago it happened this way. I lay down in my wickiup and saw a big mountain. Only I didn't know I was sleeping. It was all covered with spruce, that mountain, and I thought I really saw it. Then, on the top I saw something, so I went up, and it was a bear. I was sure scared. But then that bear talked to me. At first I didn't know what it was saying, but then I started to understand. It wasn't the words we people use around here. So it talked some more and I heard it. After that I wasn't scared. I followed it to a spring and we drank some water. Then it talked some more. I didn't say anything. Pretty soon that bear told me that if I went to a certain place I would find a black stone. That bear told me to get it. After that, the bear went away. And I tried to follow it but it didn't leave any tracks. Then I woke up. I was sure scared when I knew what I had been dreaming. I wondered about it. Then, in the morning, I went over to the place where that dream I had told me to get the stone. I found it right away, and then I knew that I could get some of that "Bear Power."

The Apache claim that persons to whom powers have been offered in dreams may refuse them. But this happens very rarely, if at all, owing to the firm belief that such an action would surely offend the power and perhaps prompt it to retaliate by causing harm.

It is interesting to note that a similar kind of thinking applies to the conduct of relationships with human beings. Whenever an Apache is presented with a gift, he is obliged to accept it, whatever its intrinsic worth. Otherwise, he would give insult and, as a result, run the risk of angering someone and being maligned in gossip. This is another example of the way in which rules for successful social interaction are paralleled by rules for maintaining amicable relations with powers.

Initial contact between a power and its future owner may also take place during the waking state. Some unusual or unexpected event, such as those described below, may be interpreted as a sign that a power is close at hand and is prepared to make itself available.

> Over there at Gleason Flat, one time, I was working cattle. That day was sure hot. Then, just when I was looking in that brush country for some cow, it started to rain. Sure rain hard. So I went with my horse under a tree. Right then some lightning hit about from here to that house (approximately 20 yards) and start rolling at me. I was sure scared. But then that lightning stopped and went into the ground just when it got to me. Then, another lightning did just like that. Come at me and go into the ground. After that I thought about it. When I got back to Cibecue, I started learning songs. I knew that power ("Lightning Power") wanted me to use it.

> My father told me this way. One time water was killing all his corn. Too much rain. All the time rain. So he didn't know if his corn would make it to the time of picking and get ripe. Then, that same day, some more clouds start coming. Just like before with a lot of rain. When those clouds got

close, he called to them: "Go away, go away." And that day it didn't rain. He did it again, the same way. Those clouds came again and he told them to take the rain away. So his corn didn't die.

After that, I guess he thought about it. He said: "Rain was listening when I called to it." So then he knew it would work for him. So he went to a medicine man and bought songs for it.

On rare occasions, an Apache may hear a voice (or voices) talking to him and attribute it to a power. Such an occurrence is considered uncommon, but it is not construed as the result of heightened perception, such as might accompany a vision or hallucination. To the Apache, powers are alive, capable of intelligible speech, and free to intrude upon the human scene whenever they wish. Distortion of the normal senses is not viewed as a prerequisite for communicating with them.

YOU FIND POWER. As mentioned earlier, the second route to the acquisition of power is not predicated on prior contact with it, or "offers," of any kind. An individual simply decides he wants to own a power, chooses one, and sets about learning the appropriate chants and prayers. In most cases a power acquired in this fashion will go to work immediately. But, occasionally, it fails to respond. This is a sign that it is not yet pleased with its prospective owner and needs time to make certain he is worthy. Months, even years, may go by before the power gives some sort of assistance. Only then—and not before—does the Apache know that he has truly acquired it.

Chants and the Cost of Acquiring Power

Each power is associated with a corpus of chants and prayers that bear its name and which, according to myth, was given to the Western Apache in the far distant past "just after earth was set up." Chants and prayers are said to "belong" to a power; they are also described as being "part" of it. In fact, the relationship between the two is so close that the term *diyi?* may be used either in reference to a power itself or to its associated chants (more commonly known as *si*). Thus, a statement such sa "X *biyi? ncahi*" ("X, his power, strong") may be interpreted in either of the following ways: (1) "X has strong power." In effect, the power X possesses is potent; (2) "X controls his power with skill and effectiveness." That is, regardless of the potency of X's power, the chants and prayers with which he manipulates it allow him to exploit fully its potential.

One or two Apaches in Cibecue claim they can control their power without chants; prayers and spoken instructions suffice. However, most people believe that chants are essential. This is especially true of medicine men, whose effectiveness in ceremonials rests squarely on their ability to "sing" to their power in such a way that it feels disposed to make diagnoses and aid in cures. One man commented on the matter by saying:

I heard it that some of these people who own it (power) just talk to it. I don't believe it, what they say. Our songs come from those things (the powers) and go back to them when we sing them. They give the songs to the people and we give them back. That way, a power knows you are trying to tell it something. It knows that when it hears songs. That is why these people sing at dances. When a power hears its songs then it will want to listen. If you don't sing songs, a power won't know where to find you, and it won't want to work for you.

Mastering chants and prayers is a difficult and time-consuming task. Chants, in particular, are extremely intricate, and since instruction in them is wholly verbal it may involve weeks and months of sustained concentration. The usual procedure is for an instructor—usually a medicine man—and the person he is teaching to live together, alone, and at some distance from other people. Under these circumstances, they can work undisturbed.

An Apache who wishes to acquire chants must be prepared to pay for them. To begin with, he must support himself and his teacher throughout the entire period of instruction. This means plenty of food and, not infrequently, a generous supply of beer and wine. Then, too, the instructor must be paid, the size of his fee depending on the number of chants he "sells" and the length of time required to teach them. In pre-reservation times payment was rendered in the form of horses, saddles, blankets, and so forth, but today money is preferred.

To get some idea of the economic investment involved in learning chants, we may look at the case of W. G., a man from Cibecue, who in 1961 decided to acquire "Horse Power." He did not wish to use it in ceremonials and learned only twelve chants. His instruction required five weeks, during which time he spent approximately $100 on groceries for himself and the medicine man who was teaching him. In addition, he paid the latter $75, one yearling heifer, and a 30-30 rifle. Total expenses exceeded $250. That year W. G., his wife, and three children, had an income of less than $1500.

It should be emphasized that W. G. learned only a few chants. A man intending to use his power in ceremonials would have learned many more—probably the entire corpus—and the price of instruction would have been proportionately greater. As time goes on, fewer and fewer Apaches acquire powers, and one of the principal reasons is the prohibitive cost of chants. For many people—especially those whose kinsmen are unwilling to help out with contributions—powers have become too expensive.

Let us now consider briefly a few of the noneconomic problems confronting an Apache who wishes to learn chants, for example, those associated with "Black-tailed Deer Power." First, he must learn the chants themselves, perhaps as many as fifty-five or sixty. This feat takes on impressive proportions when it is recognized that a single chant may consist of as many as twenty-six separate verses and require half an hour to complete. Consider, too, that practice must continue until each chant can be flawlessly performed, with every word, every line, every verse in its proper sequence. This is essential because any deviation from the fixed pattern of a chant can threaten its effectiveness and, in so doing, offend the power to which it belongs. To complicate matters further, many chants—and especially those used in curing ceremonies—make use of archaic words and phrases that differ strikingly from normal spoken Apache. Thus, in a sense, the person acquiring a power must also acquire a new language.

Just as there are rules that govern the internal structure of each individual chant, so are there rules that determine the ordering of chants in relation to each other. This syntax can get quite complicated. If, for example, we examine four chants from the Black-tailed Deer corpus, we find that chant A is allowed to precede chant B, but may never follow it. On the other hand, chant A may follow chant C but is forbidden to come before it. With respect to chant D, there are no restrictions; that is, chant A may precede or follow it or be omitted entirely. With only four chants the number of before-and-after combinations that must be learned is twelve. With a corpus of fifty chants the number is 2450.

In addition to mental agility and a tenacious memory, the acquisition of a corpus of chants requires sheer physical strength. Chants are not easy to sing. They are apt to range over more than one octave and sometimes involve abrupt and difficult changes in pitch and tempo. Then, too, they should be sung with as much volume as the singer can muster so the power to whom the chants belong will know that the singer, like itself, is strong. In short, the performance of even one chant requires considerable effort. When we take into account that it can span thirty minutes, and that a full day of practice may involve the singing of at least a dozen chants, it is no wonder that persons acquiring a power sometimes find themselves close to exhaustion.

In view of the effort and expense involved in acquiring a power, one might be prompted to ask if the benefits outweigh the costs. Most Apaches would say yes and, indeed, one does not have to look far to see that owning a power can be advantageous. Confident in its ability to aid and protect him, an Apache with a power feels unusually well equipped to cope with life's hardships and uncertainties. He has, very definitely, "something extra" on his side and consequently is apt to experience a freedom from anxiety and a heightened sense of personal security that individuals without a power lack. Then, too, a power places in the hands of its owner a valuable means to achieved status. If he uses it prudently, to benefit others, and in such a way as to avoid all suspicion of witchcraft, he will quickly reach a position from which he can demand, and receive, widespread respect. Finally, if an Apache manipulates his power effectively in ceremonials, his services as a medicine man will be sought after and well paid for. More important, his expertise in curing becomes a source of personal satisfaction and community pride.

In most cases, Apaches are pleased when someone acquires a power, for they see it as an event from which everyone in the community stands to benefit. The person who controls power functions as a vital link between two realms—the realm of self-mobile things, including man, and the realm of things that are "holy." When relations between the inhabitants of these realms go awry, only someone with power can repair the damage and restore the original balance.

4

Curing Ceremonials

Sickness and Taboos

EVERYWHERE people get sick. But cultural definitions of sickness, its causes, and how best to treat it, exhibit striking diversity. It is a fundamental postulate of Western Apache culture that serious illness can be the direct result of behaving "without respect" towards things that are *godiyo* ("holy"). More specifically, sickness occurs when an Apache violates one or more of the taboos surrounding objects from which power derives or in which it has come to reside.

One must not, for example, boil the stomach of a deer, nor eat its tongue, nor sever the tail from its hide. Wood from trees struck by lightning should not be used in cooking fires. It is dangerous to fan a fire with one's hat, or to allow the hairs combed from a horse's tail to touch the ground. One should avoid stepping on the trail left by a snake. In the morning, when the sun is rising, water used the night before should not be thrown toward the east. One must not urinate in water, nor defecate near a cornfield.

Taboos of this sort number in the hundreds. Many pertain only to men and the activities they customarily perform; others have relevance only to women. But all have one thing in common: they serve to define "respectful" and, in Apache terms, "safe" behavior toward the sources of power.

A few taboos have clear-cut practical value, and several encourage the avoidance of real sources of danger. However, the vast majority do not. It is doubtful that by observing taboos an Apache significantly reduces his chances of getting sick. But he does reduce the *fear* of getting sick and, in a society where there are many other things to cause concern, this counts for a great deal. Arbitrary as taboos may appear to the outsider, they are construed by the Apache as a set of more or less reasonable rules which exist for his own protection. To obey them is simply to demonstrate good sense. Occasionally, one hears Apaches who are cronically ill described as being "crazy" (*dogoyạda*). The implication is that only someone slightly deranged or extremely foolish would repeatedly violate taboos.

If observing taboos can help allay anxiety, the fear of violating them can help to generate it. There are many, many taboos, and I have yet to meet an Apache who claims knowledge of them all. Thus, although a man may observe assiduously the taboos with which he is familiar, the possibility always exists that he may violate one he knows nothing about. (Only when he falls ill, and a medicine man is called in for diagnosis, does he discover for certain what it is.) Equally troubling to Apaches is the fear of breaking taboos through simple negligence or carelessness. It is difficult, they explain, to always monitor what one is doing and sometimes, unintentionally and inadvertently, slip-ups occur.

Despite the worry they can cause, taboos are accepted by Apaches as a necessary and irrevocable part of their lives. Order in the universe, which all agree is desirable, is most likely to prevail when the relations between men and powers are free of hostility and typified by "respect." The same conditions hold for the maintenance and preservation of good health. The Apache worries about taboos and tries not to break them because he sees it as contributing to his own survival.

A more precise idea of how the Apache conceptualize disease causation can be gained by looking at the way they classify illnesses. At a very general level, all illnesses are partitioned into two broad categories: *nɛzkai* ("nonincapacitating illnesses") and *kasʊtị* ("incapacitating illnesses") (see Figure 7). The former term describes symptoms which are not severe enough to make the afflicted individual alter or discontinue his normal activities; the latter labels those which force him to suspend his daily routine and take to his bed.

According to whether or not they are caused by a power, incapacitating illnesses are partitioned into two subcategories. One, *kasʊtị diyɩˀ bił*, includes only those which result from a power entering the body. The second category, *kasʊtị, dodiyɩˀda*, encompasses illnesses which stem from other causes, such as "intense cold" (*dikəs*), "bad food" (*čiyən nčǫ*), and "ghosts" (*čidn*).

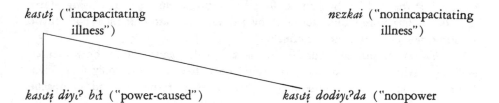

kasʊtị ("incapacitating illness")

nɛzkai ("nonincapacitating illness")

kasʊtị diyɩˀ bił ("power-caused")

kasʊtị dodiyɩˀda ("nonpower caused")

Figure 7. Portion of Western Apache disease classification showing major classes of illness.

The Apache recognize two major varieties of *kasʊtị diyɩˀbił* ("incapacitating power-caused illnesses"). These are:

1. *ænilnən* ("caused by eating"), which labels symptoms caused by a

power that has entered the body in solid food, for example, beef which when on the hoof was struck by lightning.

2. *idaʔən* ("caused by drinking, inhaling, or touching"), which labels symptoms caused by a power that has entered the body in any of the following ways: (a) Drinking liquid contaminated by a power-source, for example, water in which a bear has been swimming; (b) Inhaling smoke from burning wood that has been contaminated by a power-source, for example, smoke from wood on which a deer has urinated; (c) Coming into physical contact with a power-source in a manner forbidden by taboo, for example, stepping on a rattlesnake skin.

When a power enters the body, it may produce symptoms within a few days or it may lie dormant and undetected. It may remain in this state indefinitely, sometimes for several years. At any time, however, it can activate itself and then, suddenly and without warning, the signs of sickness appear. In either instance, the sick person must choose between two courses of action. He may do nothing, in which case his illness may get worse and conceivably prove fatal, or he may seek diagnosis and treatment in the context of ceremonials.

The Structure of Ceremonials

In the past, the ceremonial system of the Western Apache may have approached that of the Navaho in complexity. At least there is evidence to suggest that the number of distinct rituals involved was probably comparable. Most of these, it appears, were connected with curing or the bestowal of "protection" (*ɪnkɪzi*) against illness. But several, including a very important set of ceremonials relative to warfare and raiding, were held for other purposes. Today, many of the old ceremonials are no longer performed, a fact which is connected both to their high cost and to the relatively few Apaches who are presently acquiring power.

Although the variety of ceremonials presently performed is smaller than it was in pre-reservation times, the frequency of ceremonials is still quite high. For example, since 1960 over 225 curing rituals have been held in Cibecue alone. This is a very respectable figure, especially when we take into account that the expense of a single ceremony may be enough to send an entire family into bankruptcy, and that prior to 1964 Cibecue's population was less than 750.

A ceremonial can be most economically defined as any gathering, regardless of size or location, at which a medicine man sings chants. There are two major classes of curing ceremonial. The term *gojɪtał* labels those which begin at dusk and continue throughout the night until dawn of the following day. These are to be kept distinct from *edotał* (sometimes called *hadotał*), which start at the same time but which come to a close shortly after midnight. Differences in duration are paralleled by differences in function. The shorter ceremonials are held for diagnostic purposes only, that is, to determine what is causing the illness and to prescribe appropriate ritual treatment. The longer rites are aimed at eliminating causes.

Within the two classes of curing ceremonial, there are numerous variants. Which one is chosen depends upon the assumed cause of trouble (as revealed by diagnosis or as thought to be known from personal experience), the ability of the patient's family to pay, and the availability of a medicine man. Most curing ceremonials have one- and two-night forms, and quite often segments of these are incorporated into half-night diagnostic sessions.

Ceremonials have a very definite structure, a framework into which more or less discrete units are inserted. These units—items of ritual paraphernalia, chants and prayers—are dictated either by fixed associations or the preferences of individual medicine men. Although many of the same units are used over and over again in different ceremonials, a few are restricted to particular types. Thus, although every ceremonial has some distinctive items all its own, much of the inventory is common to all. Somewhere there is always a turquoise bead fastened to the base of an eagle feather; there is always cattail pollen (*hadntɪn*) or "holy powder." In practically every ritual, chants from the *gan*, bear, and black-tailed deer corpuses are sung, and prayers are offered to Changing Woman, water, and sun. Invariably, stress is placed on "thinking good thoughts." At the start of all major ceremonials, a relative or friend of the patient makes a speech exhorting everyone in attendance to behave in a serious manner and to avoid expressions of anger and hostility. Failure to do so may be construed by the medicine man's power as lack of "respect," thus making it reluctant to aid in the cure.

On the eve of a curing ceremonial, the usual practice is for someone, preferably a medicine man, to relate myths. These describe the origin of the ritual, together with the circumstances leading up to its first performance. Myths contain much fine ritual poetry and, when told by a skillful narrator, are capable of evoking the intensity of high drama. More important, they place Apaches in contact with the world of the past and, in so doing, underscore the relevance of traditional values and practices to the present. The old stories affirm the validity of ceremonials by saying, in effect, that because they have worked before—many, many times before—they are bound to work again.

A Curing Ceremonial

This section briefly describes a sequence of events that culminated in a curing ceremonial, held at Cibecue in the summer of 1963. There is nothing strikingly unusual about either the cremonial or the circumstances that produced it, and for present purposes, our example may be considered representative of a recurrent pattern. In focusing on a particular case, I hope to convey some of the substance of Western Apache curing ritual and, in so doing, move us toward a better appreciation of its effect.

It is nearly ten o'clock at night, and Clinton Nastagi,[1] age 45, sits motionless on a pile of blankets. A few yards away, against a backdrop of cottonwood trees and the dim silhouettes of towering rocks, a large bonfire pops and crackles. Around it, standing in groups of three or four, several dozen men talk quietly. One of them makes a joke but it prompts little laughter. From beyond the fire

---

[1] A fictitious name.

come the muffled sounds of women making tortillas. A baby is crying, and some-where, a long way from Clinton Nastagi's camp, two dogs are fighting.

Presently, two men emerge from a wickiup and walk toward the fire where they sit down on a large log. Each carries a drum made from a cast iron cooking pot, half-filled with water, and covered with a piece of buckskin. When struck, the drums produce a timbrous, deeply resonant thump. As the drummers test their instruments, another man enters the circle of firelight and moves to take a place between them. He is an older man with a face deeply lined with wrinkles. He is dressed like other Apaches, in shirt, blue denim pants, and wide-brimmed hat. But pinned to the front of his shirt is a small white eagle feather—the outward symbol of a medicine man. Seated now he turns and says something to one of the drummers. Then, cupping his hand behind his ear, he lurches slightly forward, straightens up, and with a piercing falsetto note begins to sing. Across the fire Clinton Nastagi remains motionless. Clinton has been sick for some time, and an attempt is now being made to cure him.

The events leading up to Clinton Nastagi's curing ceremonial started in the fall of the preceding year, when he went on a hunting trip with two of his friends. The men left Cibecue early one November morning and rode north. South of a spot the Apaches call *ḳiḍuklïž* ("Blue House"), Clinton dismounted his horse and started to hunt on foot. A few minutes later he shot and killed a white-tailed buck, which, in accordance with established practice, he dressed immediately. After he had wrapped the meat in a piece of canvas, he sat down against a tree to await the return of his friends. For a while he slept. What happened after that is best de-scribed in Clinton's own words.

I woke up when those two men came back. I saw them looking at me. Then I saw why they were doing it. That tree had been hit by lightning. On the side away from me there was a big black mark where it had been hit. I didn't see it. I got worried then and wondered about sleeping on that tree. I guess those two men were feeling worried for me, too, but they didn't say anything.

Clinton returned to Cibecue and went about his normal activities. His health remained good. But one night during the winter he was awakened by a bad dream. In it he saw the very same tree he had leaned against on the hunting trip get struck by lightning. And at the moment of contact he felt "something" run through his body.

After that I really got worried. I told my wife and she got scared, too. But we didn't have any money for a dance (curing ceremonial), so we didn't have one. After that I just hoped nothing bad would happen to me.

But something did. In the months that followed, Clinton was bothered by headaches and a feeling of general malaise. He quit going to work, and whenever he was able to borrow money he spent it on beer. He argued frequently with his wife and one afternoon, when intoxicated, he threatened to kill her.

After I got sober again, my wife told me what I said. I sure felt bad about it. But she never get angry with me, that woman, and said it was all right. Then, she said it: "My husband, I don't know what is in you. Sometimes you act crazy, never stay home, run around and look for drink. I don't know why your brain is hurting from something, but I think you should find out about it."

After that, I asked her to go to that old medicine man and ask him for *edotał* (a diagnostic ceremony). First she went to her sister's camp and got an eagle feather and a blue stone (turquoise). The medicine man's power needs those things. That way it knows you are serious. Then, after that—my wife went to that old man's camp, and gave him those things for power, and asked him would he sing for my trouble and find out about it. He said yes. But it would cost twenty dollars.

A diagnostic ceremonial was held at Clinton's camp two days later. Before it started the medicine man and Clinton talked informally.

I told that medicine man about lots of things. I told him about that time I went hunting and touched that tree. The dream I had, too, I told him about that. Also, I said I thought maybe it was lightning that was after me.

When the sun had gone down, the medicine man sang sixteen "lightning chants." Only a few people attended the ceremony—Clinton's wife and children, two of his sisters and their families, and three male cousins who came alone. After he had finished singing, the medicine man gave his diagnosis. He announced that, just as Clinton himself had supposed, the headaches and the bad dream were the result of coming into contact with the lightning-struck tree. The medicine man also said that a one-night "lightning ceremonial" would be necessary to effect a cure. Clinton felt relieved. "Now I know what's getting after me," he said.

Clinton and his wife spent the next six weeks getting together enough money to cover the cost of the forthcoming ceremonial. They would have to pay for a medicine man and, in addition, provide food for everyone who came. Clinton had practically no money of his own, so he went to his kinsmen, especially the members of his clan. Almost everyone he visited pledged support of one kind or another. Those who were unable (or unwilling) to contribute money promised to supply food, or help prepare it, or gather firewood. Three days before the ceremonial, Clinton and his wife had over two hundred dollars, Forty-five dollars would go to the medicine man, the same one who had diagnosed Clinton's trouble. The rest would be spent on food—coffee and sugar, flour for tortillas, baking powder, and potatoes. There would also be meat. One of Clinton's cousins, a woman who owned cattle, had promised to slaughter a heifer.

On the day of the ceremonial, Clinton's wife encouraged him to stay in his wickiup and try to sleep. He would be awake all that night, and the more rest he could get now the better. Toward dusk friends and relatives started to arrive. Some came in pick-up trucks, some on horseback. Several lived close enough to walk. Soon it was dark and someone started a fire. The medicine man was on hand. All was in readiness.

It is well past midnight, and the medicine man has been chanting steadily for over two hours. Perspiration runs down his face, under his chin, and every so often he takes a handkerchief from his pocket and mops his neck. The chant, which comes from the lightning corpus, is high-pitched and intricate in tempo. The beat of the drums is steady, almost monotonous. Standing behind the medicine man and drummers are ten or twelve men who join in the chorus which follows each verse. They are not medicine men, these additional singers, nor do they necessarily own a power. But they have heard the chant many times and they enjoy singing. So much the better. "Lightning Power" will interpret it as a sign of respect.

The chant comes to an end. Waiting until the last notes have lost themselves in the night, the medicine man rises and walks stiffly in the direction of Clinton Nastagi's wickiup. Inside there is food and hot coffee. For the medicine man there is a small bucket of *tułpai*, a native liquor made from fermented corn. The midpoint in the ceremony has been reached, and now it is time for everyone to rest and eat. For the next few hours there is little activity. Small children, worn out from wrestling and games of tag, sleep on the ground wrapped in blankets. Adults talk idly. Even the dogs—ubiquitous at large gatherings—are quiet. Clinton Nastagi drinks coffee to stay awake.

It is close to three o'clock when the curing ceremonial resumes. The fire, which has been allowed to die down, is replenished. Once again the medicine man and the drummers take their places. The chants begin: four more from the lightning corpus, two from the *gan*, four from black-tailed deer. There is a pause while the medicine man drinks some *tułpai*. Then, more chants.

With the first light of dawn, the singing stops. Picking up a small basket filled with cattail pollen, the medicine man walks to where Clinton Nastagi is sitting. He sprinkles pollen on each of Clinton's shoulders and on the top of his head. Next he takes from the basket a piece of "lightning grass" and touches it to Clinton's forehead. This action, it is believed, will neutralize the "Lightning Power" in Clinton's brain. The pollen blessing is then repeated.

Wearily the medicine man returns to his seat and, in a voice grown hoarse, sings two final chants. The ceremonial is over, and people prepare to leave. Clinton gets up from his pile of blankets and walks slowly to his wickiup. He lies down on his bed and goes instantly to sleep.

The Effects of Curing Ceremonials

What does a curing ceremonial do for a Western Apache like Clinton Nastagi?

The principal message is probably one of reassurance. Long before the ceremony takes place—in fact, directly after diagnosis—the patient hears from the medicine man and others that he will be cured. Prior to the ceremony, myths reiterate the same theme. And during the actual proceedings, those in attendance are instructed to think only "good thoughts" and to talk of health and longevity.

The crowd at a ceremonial is usually composed of nearly all the persons who have been of importance in the patient's life—his relatives, his friends, what one writer has termed "the human guideposts who have formed his orientation in the world." These same individuals, the patient knows, have cared enough to help him, to contribute tangibly toward his continued well-being. They have focused attention on him, they have worried about him. They want to see him well again.

There is also the prestige and authority of the medicine man who, by his very presence and esoteric knowledge, assures the patient that everything possible is being done to bring about his recovery.

The considerable investment that a patient (and his kinsmen) must make to have a ceremonial may well contribute to the feeling that positive results will be obtained. Like ourselves, Apaches are reluctant to think that anything that has cost them time and money is a failure.

Finally, it is very likely that the patient has witnessed the ceremonial before and has seen it work for others. This, too, will give him confidence. Perhaps, as the myths suggest, he will view his predicament in the context of an unbroken chain of similar events that stretches back to the beginning of time—to the time when the very ceremonial from which he now stands to benefit was first bestowed upon his ancestors.

As well as reassurance, ceremonials provide people like Clinton Nastagi with diversion and occupation. From the moment the decision is made to have a ceremonial, the patient devotes himself to it completely. He must find money with which to pay a medicine man. He must see to it that there is a plentiful supply of food. He must coordinate the activities of others so that everything is ready at the proper time. In short, the Apache patient does not lie helpless before a cruel and impersonal fate. Throughout the period of preparation, he is actively engaged in doing something about his own misfortune.

The primary effects of Western Apache curing ceremonials are psychological. There should be nothing too mysterious about this. Skillful physicians have known for a long time that the will to get well, and the belief that one is going to recover, can be more than half the battle. Furthermore, the fact that many physical disabilities stem from psychic disorders is by now well established. Western Apache curing practices reinforce in a number of ways the patient's own desire to be cured. In so doing they relieve anxiety and tension, instill a sense of security, and render him better able to bear his illness. In the words of one Apache, curing ceremonials give "good hope."

5

The Girls' Puberty Ceremony

URING RITUALS constitute the bulk of Western Apache ceremonialism but by no means the whole of it. Minor ceremonies are held at childbirth, at the start of long and difficult journeys, at planting and harvest time and, occasionally, upon the completion of a newly constructed wickiup or house. Moreover, there is a considerable amount of essentially private ritual carried out in connection with the manipulation of powers. But of all Western Apache ceremonials, that which is performed on the most elaborate scale and which affects directly the greatest number of people is the girls' puberty rite. This ceremony is ostensibly given to invest a young girl with those qualities Apaches consider essential for adulthood but, in fact, it does a great deal more and has consequences of singular importance for the entire community.

The puberty rite differs from other Western Apache ceremonials in several respects, but most conspicuously in the amount and richness of its symbolism. In what follows we will describe this symbolism and attempt to explain it in ways consistent with the interpretations of native informants. With a knowledge of what the puberty rite means to Apaches, that is, how *they* appraise the objects and acts which comprise it, the significance of the ceremony will be easier to understand.

Preliminaries

At one point in history, probably no more than fifty years ago, almost every Western Apache girl had a puberty ceremony, or *nai²es* ("preparing her"; "getting her ready"). Today this is no longer true. In Cibecue the ceremony is performed only two or three times a year, and in a number of other settlements on the Fort Apache Reservation, it is not held at all. Two reasons for this decline are readily apparent. First, as a result of increased contact with white and Indian missionaries who strongly criticize the "old way religion," younger Apaches have come to doubt the effectiveness of *nai²es*—that it will assure the pubescent girl, among other things, of long life and prosperity. A second reason that the ceremonial is held less and less is its prohibitive cost. As will become evident below, the expense in money and labor far surpasses what most people are able, or willing, to afford.

The decision to hold the puberty ceremony is usually made before a girl has her first menses. If, as sometimes happens, parents are hesitant, a grandparent may supply the incentive. One man recalled:

> I wasn't sure about having a dance. My wife wanted to because she had one when she was a girl. Now, some people think it's old-fashioned and the medicine men don't have the power. It costs a lot, too. We don't know what to do. Then it came close to when my daughter was to bleed for the first time, so we had to get going. Then my mother came to my camp and said, "I hear you won't give my granddaughter *nai²es*. Why don't you have her one? I am an old lady but I am still strong. *Nai²es* did that." We decided it was good to have *nai²es*.

A girl's parents will not contemplate *nai²es* unless they think they can afford it. In addition, relations between members of the girl's family and their consanguineal kinsmen must be unstrained because, without the contributions of the latter, there would be too much work for an extended family, even a large one, to accommodate. One informant commented on this problem as follows:

> When I have *nai²es* for my daughter, I had trouble at first. A lot of people were mad at my wife because she got drunk one night and got into a fight with my brother's wife. She hit her with a bottle and had to go to jail in Whiteriver for sixty days. They said to me: "We won't help you get ready for *nai²es* because your wife drinks too much and acts crazy." Even my clan relatives were mad. They said: "Why does your wife fight with your brother's wife? He has been friendly with her. It is because she drinks all the time. Maybe she would get drunk and fight with us." I was really scared for a while, because I didn't know if anybody would help us at the dance. Then my wife apologized and cut down on drinking, and we got help. But some people were still mad, and did nothing for us.

Occasionally nonrelatives offer to help, particularly when the dance ground is being prepared. But it is rare for persons who are not related in some way to one or more members of the girl's extended family to take a large part in the preliminaries. Said one Apache:

> Relatives do most of the work, but sometimes friends help out. They know it's good to help, and they might get some food for helping. A friend of mine let me use his pick-up three times to haul groceries from Whiteriver. My wife borrowed two baskets from her friend. Neither of these people are related to us, but they just wanted to help out. When they get the place ready and have social dancing until midnight, young men come and work during the day. They go to the dance at night. I guess that's why they do it.

If, for one reason or another, the pubescent girl does not want to have *nai²es*, she makes her feelings known and, if they persist, plans for the ceremony are dropped. The father of one unwilling girl observed:

My daughter didn't want a dance. She said she was bashful and that her friends would tease her. So my wife talked to her, but she didn't change her mind. My wife and my wife's parents were sure mad. We never had the dance. It wouldn't be good to make her have the dance if she didn't want it.

Actual preparations for *nai*ʔ*es* are not begun until after the girl has her first period. With her consent to participate willingly in the ceremony, enough money (or promises of it) to finance a large portion of the expenses, and good relations with kinsmen, the girl's parents are ready to proceed in earnest.

"WISE PEOPLE" (*nde guyane*). Immediately after a girl's first menstruation, her parents select a group of older people, called *nde guyane*, with whom it is decided when and where the ceremony will be held and, most important, who will serve as the girl's "sponsor" (*naiɫʔesn*).

The problem of selecting a date is not a difficult one, for regardless of when the girl has her first period, *nai*ʔ*es* is held in late June, July, or August. Apaches give two main reasons for preferring the summer months. First, the evenings and nights are warm, and second, more people—notably boarding-school students home on vacation—are able to attend.

Once a date has been selected, a site for the ceremonial must be decided upon. Necessary requisites include an abundant source of water close at hand; proximity to a large supply of wood; and ample space for temporary dwellings. If the girl's own camp is lacking, a location is chosen outside the settlement. One woman, who had given *nai*ʔ*es* for her daughter, recalled:

> Our camp was no good for *nai*ʔ*es*. It wasn't big enough to have a dance, and there wasn't flat ground there. So we had it at "where the road crosses the creek." That was a good place. There weren't many stones or weeds there and it was easy to make a place to dance. Trees were so we could use them as part of the shades and the places we kept the *tuɫpai* and groceries. Another thing was that the cattle were close to that place so it was easy to get them to be butchered.

The *nde guyane* must also select a medicine man. Here, a unique problem faces the people of Cibecue because there are no living medicine men in the settlement who control the power required for puberty ceremonials. Therefore, a medicine man must be secured from elsewhere. Once a candidate has been agreed upon, it remains for the girl's father to visit him and ask him to conduct the ceremonial. Taking along an eagle feather and turquoise, cattail pollen, and enough money to pay the medicine man's fee, he sets out before sunrise.

> I got there real early and waited in my pick-up until the sun came up. I didn't see anything so I just sat there. Then his wife came out of her wickiup and threw some water away she had in a cooking pot. She saw the truck but she didn't say anything and went back inside. Then the medicine man came out and went behind the wickiup to make water. When he came back I got out of my truck and went to where he was. I took all the stuff with me that I would give him. He had sung *nai*ʔ*es* for my daughter four years ago, so I already knew him and how much he would charge. When I got to where he was sitting he held out his left hand, inside (palm) up. He held it like this

and I opened the jar and took out some powder. I made a cross with it on his hand in the four directions. Then I took out $50 from my wallet and put it in his hand. Then I said, "Will you sing *nai?es* for my daughter?" He said, "Yes." Then I told him what day it was (to be held) and he said that was good and that he would be there 2 days early, so to have everything ready then. Then he put the $50 in his pocket. I went home after that and told *nde guyane* what he said. They were glad he said yes and would sing.

SELECTION OF A "SPONSOR" (*naiɬ?esn*). The most important decision confronting *nde guyane* is the selection of a woman to act as sponsor for the pubescent girl. This woman plays a vital role in the ceremony and, in addition, is expected to make a large financial contribution. The principal criterion governing her selection is that she belong neither to the clan of the pubescent girl, nor to the clan of the girl's father, nor to any clan to which these two are "closely related," "related," or "distantly related" (see Chapter 1: Social Organization). Let us recall that a clan is composed of persons who consider themselves related through matrilineal descent, and that every clan has imputed matrilineal relationships with other clans which, together, comprise a clan set. Restating the above proscription in these terms, a sponsor must come from a clan which is not related to any clan in the girl's clan set or to any clan in her father's clan set (see Figure 8).

Once the *nde guyane* have singled out all women who are eligible by clan for the role of sponsor, they make their final decision on the basis of good character and wealth. Ideally, a sponsor should be someone of spotless reputation; the following statements indicate some of the qualities on which such reputations are commonly based.

> *Naiɬ?esn* must be a good person. She must be strong and work hard and never be lazy. Also she shouldn't drink too much or act crazy. She shouldn't say mean things that will make other people mad at her and fight with her. . . . must be friendly with people and not make them fight with her. She should be pretty old and wise about things. All the time she says nice things to people.
>
> . . . It's good if she had a *nai?es* when she was a girl herself. That way she is wise and knows about the things in *nai?es,* and it makes her strong and healthy and easy to get along with. If she had *nai?es* she won't act crazy or drink too much or get in trouble or bother people. That's why it is best to get someone who had *nai?es* to be *naiɬ?esn.*
>
> . . . should not be sick very much but strong so she can work hard and made a good clean camp. It's good if she has lots of children. Part of *nai?es* is so the girl has children easily and won't die (in childbirth).

The procedure of asking a woman to act as sponsor is patterned on that of requesting the services of a medicine man. The father of the pubescent girl (or someone appointed to speak on his behalf) visits the woman's camp before sunrise and asks her to assume the role. If she accepts, she is given an eagle feather and cattail pollen. This is a very important event, for it inaugurates a formal relationship between the pubescent girl, her parents, and the sponsor and her husband—a relationship that is binding for life, and one which is marked by the adoption of hitherto unused terms of address. Henceforth, the girl and her parents

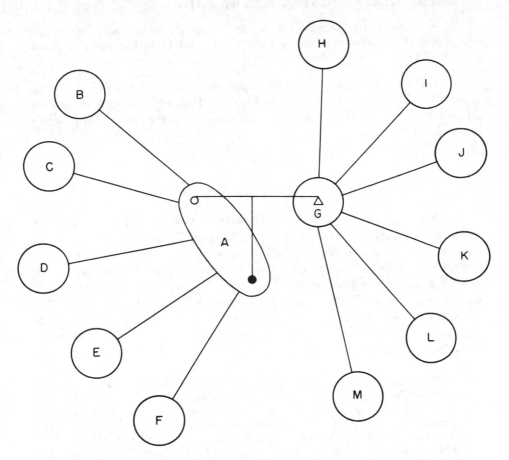

Figure 8. Clan Relationships. The pubescent girl's clan (and her mother's clan) is clan A, which is related to clan B-F. Clans A-F make up the girl's clan set. The girl's father's clan is clan G which is related to clans H-M. Clans G-M make up his clan set. The pubescent girl's sponsor must come from a clan which is not related to any of the clans in these two clan sets.

may call the sponsor and her husband by the term *šɪtɪke* ("my very close friend"), and vice versa. By extension, *šɪtɪke* means "all that I have you may consider yours," and this principle sets the tone for a new set of reciprocal obligations incumbent on the persons involved. Reduced to essentials, they are expected to aid each other for whatever reason and whenever the need may arise. The significance of the *šɪtɪke* relationship lies in the fact that Apaches consider it every bit as demanding as those based on matrilineal kinship. Said one informant:

> When you call someone *šɪtɪke* you always help him out. It's good to have someone like that because he will help you. When my baby girl died last year, the woman who was my wife's *naiłʔesn* sure helped us out. She gave us food and made her brother kill a beef for us. My wife gives her presents now and then too. Last year I think my wife gave her some cloth for a dress. Whenever you get in trouble it's good to have someone like that. There was

a man who had a son who got put in jail in Whiteriver on a fornication charge. The woman who was *naiʔesn* for that man's daughter gave him some money to help bail the boy out of jail.

Like the pubescent girl's parents, a sponsor prepares for *naiʔes* by relying heavily on the support of matrilineal kinsmen. Her major task is to procure enough food to give the girl and her relatives a large feast on the day before the ceremonial.

Preparations

Apaches attach considerable importance to ceremonial preparations, and negligence in carrying them out is viewed with alarm. To a large extent the effectiveness of a ritual is thought to depend upon its being performed in precise coincidence with established pattern. Anything that disturbs or alters this pattern may be construed by a power as signifying lack of "respect." It is important to view the elaborate preparations that accompany ceremonials as the Apaches do. Precautions are taken against the occurrence of incidents, which would inject an unexpected and unwelcome element of disorder into a ceremony and, in so doing, threaten its success. One Apache said:

> Everything should be ready before it starts. You shouldn't have to do any work while it's going on. There should be enough food and *tuɫpai* for everybody, and the place should be clean. I was at a sing one time and they hadn't cleaned up the place. There were bottles and paper and tin cans lying around. The medicine man picked up a can and threw it away real hard. He was mad because the place wasn't clean. He sang but he was mad. They should have cleaned up.

THE DANCEGROUND. As mentioned earlier, a puberty ceremonial may be held at the girl's own camp or, if this location is unsatisfactory, elsewhere. At a site beyond the community, from four to nine structures are erected. These include a semi-permanent wickiup for the pubescent girl and members of her family, large shades (or ramadas) in which food will be prepared, and smaller shelters for the storage of groceries and clothing. Characteristically, these structures are built in two separate groups, some distance apart and usually facing each other across the danceground (see Figure 9). One group will be used by the sponsor and her kinsmen, the other by relatives of the pubescent girl. All preparations are in the hands of the latter, and the sponsor is not expected to arrive at the site until the shades and food shelters have been completed.

The following account gives a detailed description of preparations for a puberty ceremonial and indicates clearly the various stages through which the work progresses.

> I took my family up there and the first night we slept in tents. The next day my son and me and my wife made a big wickiup for my family. It had to be big because I have lots of children. When that was finished, it was good

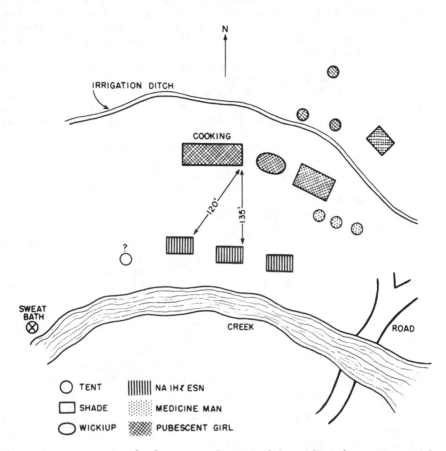

Figure 9. Western Apache danceground prepared for girl's puberty ceremonial.

for the whole family. The next day, two of my brothers came up there and so did my wife's father and my parents. The brothers didn't spend the night, but the old people did, and they moved into the tents we had been using before. We didn't do much that day. After that, when my brothers came back, we started building a big shade for cooking and making *tułpai*. It sure was a big one—we had lots to do. We had to get long posts and there weren't any close by, so my son and two brothers took my pickup and went to get some up by White Springs. They cut down a lot of trees and made them the right length and brought them back. Then we made the shade. The men put in the posts and made the top and the women made the sides mostly. It sure took us a long time to make that shade. About a week, I think. We didn't do it all alone because some more relatives came and helped us out. My wife's brother and his wife came, and so did my sister and her husband. They didn't have to come. I didn't ask them. But they sure wanted to help me out. All those people went home at night but they came back in the morning. We always gave them some food and *tułpai* when they finished working. When that big shade was all over, we started on food shelters. They're easy to make, because you don't need big logs for posts. We made two of them in about two days, but we took it easy. After that we brought some food up there. We didn't bring all we bought for *nai²es*. About this time my cross-cousin went to see what yearlings we should butcher. He and some others got them and put them in the bull pasture by Cowboy Springs. We didn't butcher until two days before *nai²es* so we left them there.

Our camp was finished up there and more people came to help us make shades for *naił²esn*. We built them on the other side of the dance area from where ours were. It's usually like this when you have *nai²es* out of Cibecue. I don't know why it is. We made a big shade for *naił²esn* to stay in and a big shade for cooking too. That shade wasn't as big as ours because they don't have so many people to help with cooking. After we made these my cross-cousin said we should build another one because *naił²esn* had lots of people coming with her. So we did. Over there we didn't make food shelters. Just covered-over places inside the shades. That took a long time and we sure had to get a lot of wood. All along other people helped. My brother came from Whiteriver with his son. He only stayed two days but his son didn't go home. My wife's brother came too. He's pretty old but he can still work hard. He is still strong. He didn't stay there at night, but we gave him food and *tułpai* when he went home. After that, I went to *naił²esn's* camp (in Cibecue) and told her that we were ready. She came there the next day with her husband and about twenty other people. They were her relatives. I knew most of them because they live in Cibecue, but some had come from San Carlos.

Then we had a lot of people up there, and the work got a little easier. We cleared away all the weeds and stones from where they would sing and dance. We needed lots of firewood and the men did that with pick-ups. The women put the food and candy away and made *tułpai*. Pretty soon everything was ready. All we had to do was make a tent for the medicine man and we did that two days before he came up there from Cedar Creek. One night everybody got drunk and my cousin got into a fight with a boy from San Carlos. He didn't get hurt and we stopped the fight. I went and got groceries twice from Show Low and once from Whiteriver. We had lots of flour and coffee and sugar and potatoes. So we were just about ready. Two days before *nai²es*, I went to Cedar Creek and got the medicine man and his wife.

The Day before *Nai²es*

On the day before a puberty ceremonial, two important events take place. In order of their occurrence, these are:

1. "Cane, it is made" (*gišižaha²alde*)—a sweatbath, attended by male relatives of the pubescent girl and her sponsor, at which the medicine man fashions ritual paraphernalia for the forthcoming ceremonial.

2. "Food, exchanged" (*niła²ika*)—the presentation, by the sponsor to the pubescent girl, of a large quantity of food and groceries.

RITUAL PARAPHERNALIA. As we shall see, the most important quality bestowed on the pubescent girl during *nai²es* is longevity. This is symbolized by a decorated wooden staff (*gišižaha*) with which she dances throughout the ceremony and which, years later, she may use as a walking stick.

Girl's puberty ceremonial: Phase VII. (Pubescent girl is on left; white substance in her hair is cattail pollen used for blessings) Cibecue 1964.

Girl's puberty ceremonial: Phase II. (Pubescent girl is on left, her sponsor on right) Cibecue 1964.

Drinking tułpai at girl's puberty ceremonial, Cibecue 1962.

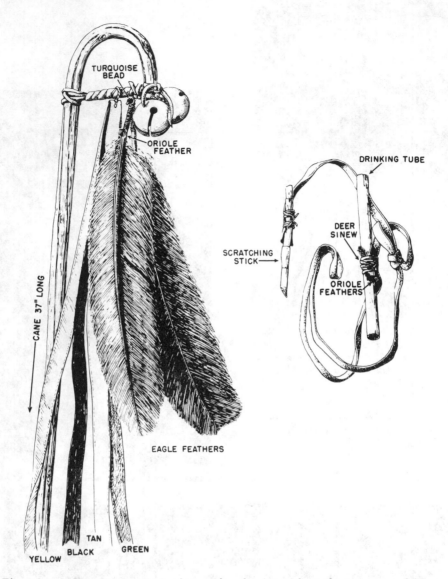

TURQUOISE BEAD

ORIOLE FEATHER

CANE 37" LONG

DRINKING TUBE

SCRATCHING STICK →

DEER SINEW

ORIOLE FEATHERS

EAGLE FEATHERS

TAN

BLACK GREEN

YELLOW

Figure 10. Major items of ritual paraphenelia for girl's puberty ceremonial.

At *nai?es*, she dances with that to make her live many years. After *nai?es* she keeps it at her camp and when she gets to be an old woman, and has trouble walking long ways, she uses it to help her out.

The staff is painted yellow and may vary in length from 32 to 50 inches. A male relative of the pubescent girl secures a straight piece of wood, strips off the bark, and creates a crook by bending over one end and fastening it securely with a rawhide thong. Next, the medicine man covers the cane with a mixture of yellow ochre and water. When the paint is dry, he ties two eagle feathers to the rawhide thong. To the base of one feather a turquoise bead is attached; to the other, two small feathers taken from a species of oriole. The eagle feathers symbolize protection against power-caused illnesses. The oriole feathers are symbolic of a good disposition (see Figure 10).

Of all birds, Apaches believe the oriole gets along best with members of his own kind. This quality is also highly valued in humans. As one man put it:

> It never says bad words, that bird, and tries to be happy all the time. It always talks good, and minds its own business and never gets into fights. Every day the same way with that bird. Always acting good. Those feathers on her stick make that girl be just that way—always act good. That is how it should be with everybody.

Two other items of singular importance are *tube²iłtłəne* ("drinking tube") and *bi²adıčık* ("scratching stick"). The drinking tube is fashioned from the stalk of a cattail plant; it is about 2 inches long and painted yellow like the cane. The scratching stick, somewhat longer and also covered with ochre, is pointed at one end and may be carved on the other. Both items are attached to a strip of rawhide which, during the ceremony, the pubescent girl wears around her neck. Throughout *nai²es*, and for four days thereafter, the girl is instructed to drink only through the tube and scratch herself only with the stick. Were she to drink from a container, it is believed, she would develop unsightly facial hair. If she touched herself with her fingers, ugly sores would appear and mar her complexion. As interpreted by Apaches, then, the drinking tube and scratching stick are symbolic of physical beauty.

Other articles of ritual paraphernalia include:

1. A small pendant of abalone shell which will identify the pubescent girl as *istanadlẹ̀žẹ* ("White Shell Woman"; "Changing Woman"), a mythological figure whose power is invoked during the puberty ceremonial.

2. An eagle feather which will be fastened to the girl's hair in such a way that it hangs down behind her. Like the cane, the eagle feather symbolizes longevity; it is white or gray, and Apaches explain that it will cause the girl to live until her hair turns a similar color.

3. A buckskin sarape, fringed and beaded, which the medicine man covers with yellow ochre. To each of its shoulders he attaches a small, downy eagle feather. These, it is said, will enable the girl to walk and run as lightly as feathers float on air.

4. A large, tanned buckskin on which the pubescent girl will dance. The buckskin symbolizes a plentiful supply of meat and assures that the girl will never know hunger.

"FOOD, EXCHANGED" (*niła²ika*). When work on the ritual paraphernalia is finished, the sponsor presents the pubescent girl and her kinsmen with enough food for a large feast. And on the following day, after *nai²es* has ended, the girl's relatives reciprocate. These events formally join the sponsor and the members of her family with those of the pubescent girl in the supposedly everlasting *šıtıke* relationship. By exchanging food, the fundamental premise of *šıtıke*—"all that I have may be considered yours"—is symbolically acted out.

Nai^ɂes

The girls' puberty rite is the only major Apache ceremonial that is not performed at night. Shortly before sunrise, a large tarpaulin is spread on the ground near the center of the danceground, and eight or twelve blankets piled on top. The buckskin is then placed on the uppermost blanket, its anterior end pointing towards the east. Next, six or eight cardboard cartons filled with candy, chewing gum, and fruit are arranged in two rows directly in front of the buckskin. Finally, two small baskets—one containing cigarettes, the other cattail pollen—and four drums are set in an arc to the west.

Before the ceremonial begins, a male relative of the pubescent girl walks to the center of the danceground and addresses everyone present.

It is time that you should all be awake. Pretty soon *nai^ɂes* will start up. Don't be lazy. We want you all to see this dance. It will be a good one. Everybody should behave real good, and don't get into any trouble. Wear good clothes and get real clean. Don't drink too much or make any disturbance. We have spent a lot on this dance and we want you to like it. So do us a favor and don't get into trouble. And watch out for your children. There will be lots of people milling around and driving their trucks. Last week over at Canyon Day a little boy got run over because his mother wasn't watching he was behind a truck. Don't let that happen here, please. We want everyone to have a good time. I have said what I have said.

When the speech is over, the medicine man and four drummers take places behind the buckskin. As the first chant begins, the pubescent girl, clad in her buckskin serape and carrying the decorated cane, comes forth from her wickiup, followed by a maternal aunt or, as the case may be, an older sister. The crowd, which by this time may have grown to 600 people, closes in behind them. The girl and her relative stand on the buckskin, facing east towards the rising sun. The crowd draws closer. *Nai^ɂes* is about to begin.

"CHANGING WOMAN" (*istənadlẹ̀žẹ*). As interpreted by Apaches, the primary objective of the puberty ceremonial is to transform the pubescent girl into the mythological figure *istənadlẹ̀žẹ* ("Changing Woman"). At the request of the presiding medicine man, and "traveling on his chants," the power of Changing Woman enters the girl's body and resides there for four days. During this time, the girl acquires all the desirable qualities of Changing Woman herself, and is thereby prepared for a useful and rewarding life as an adult.

According to myth, there was a time on earth when Changing Woman lived all alone. Longing for children, she had sexual intercourse with Sun and, not long after, brought forth *nayenezgəne* ("Slayer of Monsters"), the foremost Western Apache culture hero. Four days later, Changing Woman became pregnant by water and gave birth to *tubadiscine* ("Born of Water"). As these half-brothers (or "twins") matured, Changing Woman instructed them in many things. They then left home and, making constant use of her advice, rid earth of much that was evil. Unlike certain other figures in Apache mythology, Changing Woman is never crippled by old age. As a medicine man explained it:

Changing Woman never gets too old. When she gets to be a certain age, she goes walking towards the east. After a while she sees herself in the distance walking toward her. They both walk until they come together and after that there is only one, the young one. Then she is like a young girl all over again.

The power of Changing Woman gives the pubescent girl longevity and the physical capabilities of someone perpetually young. This is the fundamental theme of *nai'es*.

Phases

As performed in Cibecue, the puberty ceremonial is composed of eight distinct parts or phases. Each phase has a name, each is initiated and terminated by a particular group of chants, and each is followed by a lengthy pause (sometimes lasting as long as twenty minutes), during which no chants are sung, and the pubescent girl is allowed to rest.

PHASE I—"ALONE, SHE DANCES" (*bildenilke*). Throughout phase I, the pubescent girl dances in place on the buckskin. With face expressionless and eyes downcast, she bounces lightly on one foot, then on the other, in time to the beat of the drums. The chants accompanying phase I deal with the Western Apache creation and emphasize the vital contributions made by Changing Woman. By the end of phase I, Changing Woman's power has entered the girl's body, and she is instructed to pray to herself: "Long life, no trouble, Changing Woman."

PHASE II—"KNEELING" (*nizta*). Shortly before the beginning of phase II, the pubescent girl's sponsor makes her first appearance of the day. Walking to the buckskin, she replaces the woman who escorted the girl during phase I. For the remainder of the ceremony, the sponsor will instruct the girl and give her moral support. Said one woman, who had filled the role of sponsor several times:

> *Naił'esn* tells the girl what to do, and not to be scared or bashful. The girl does not know what to do next and someone must tell her. That's what she (*naił'esn*) does. She doesn't have any power at all, and the reason she does that (instruct the girl) is because she helped put on the dance, and because they are not relatives..

Phase II recreates Changing Woman's impregnation by Sun. The following version of this incident was given by a medicine man from Cibecue.

> This way I heard it from my grandfather. He was from Carizzo, but they tell it always the same way over here (at Cibecue). She was living all by herself and went out one day for berries to get. It was before the Sun came up that she went out. Then when the Sun came up, she felt tired and sat down. She looked at the Sun and kneeled down like the girl does in *nai'es* in front of it. When she did that one of the Sun's red rays came and went in there. After that she noticed that she was bleeding from there and she didn't know what it meant because it was her first time. When it stopped she found out

she was pregnant. That's all I know about that part of the story. I don't think there is any more to it.

Before the start of phase II, the pubescent girl sets aside her cane and takes a kneeling position in the buckskin. As the chants begin, she raises her hands to shoulder level and, looking directly into the sun, sways from side to side. The critical fact that she has menstruated for the first time is symbolized by her assumption of the posture in which Changing Woman underwent the same experience.

PHASE III—"LYING" (*nizti*). After the pause that follows phase II, the medicine man instructs the pubescent girl to lie prone on the buckskin, with her arms at her sides and her legs together. During phase III, the girl remains in this position while her sponsor massages the muscles in her legs, back, arms, and shoulders. These actions are predicated on the belief that Changing Woman's power causes the girl's body to become soft and malleable so that, like clay, it can be molded. A medicine man explained:

Changing Woman's power is in the girl and makes her soft, like a lump of wet clay. Like clay, she can be put into different shapes. *Naiɬʔesn* puts her in the right shape and Changing Woman's power in the girl makes her grow up that way, in that same shape. When *naiɬʔesn* rubs her the right way, she will grow up strong and hard and never get tired.

Naiɬʔesn rubs her legs so she will never have any trouble walking long ways. Also, so she can stand up for long time and never get tired. She rubs her back so that when she gets to be really old age she won't bend over and not straighten up. Her shoulders . . . so she can carry heavy things for her camp and never get tired doing that either; carry wood and water and groceries long ways.

Naiɬʔesn rubs her back and legs so she can always work hard for a long time and never get tired out.

Naiɬʔesn does that for her so she will grow up strong and in good shape and always be able to help out at her camp and whenever her relatives need help.

PHASE IV—"CANE SET OUT, SHE RUNS AROUND IT" (*gišižaha yinda ɬediɬʔilye*). Prior to the start of phase IV, the pubescent girl's cane is taken from her and inserted upright in the ground about 15 yards east of the buckskin. When the first chant begins, she runs to the cane, circles it once, and runs back again. She is closely followed by her sponsor who, after going around the cane, returns with it to the buckskin. Here, she hands it to the girl, and the remainder of the chant is danced in place. This procedure is repeated during the three additional chants that comprise phase IV. At the start of each chant, the cane is placed further away from the buckskin, thereby increasing the distance the girl must run.

Each of the four runs in phase IV symbolizes a stage of life through which the pubescent girl has passed, or hopes to pass in the future. The first, and shortest, is infancy (*meʔ*). The second represents childhood and adolescence (*ǰeki*). The third run symbolizes adulthood (*istsən*), and the fourth, which is the longest, is old age (*san*). Apaches believe that as soon as the girl circles the cane, she "owns" the stage of life it stands for. Thus, after completing the final run, the girl has symbolically passed through all the stages of life and is assured of living until she is very old. A woman commented:

> For the girl, that is the most important part. That is where she prays for long life. She has the power to make herself very old when she runs around the cane that way. Each time she runs around the cane that way she will live to be that age. That way, after she makes the last time—when it is far away—she will live until a very old lady. She goes through her life running around that cane. Changing Woman did that one time and it made her very old. The girl has her power to grow up to a long age.

PHASE V—"RUNNING" (*nistan*). Phase V does not differ greatly from phase IV, and its alleged purpose is similar to that of phase III. Again the cane is set out to the east, and again the pubescent girl and her sponsor run to circle it. The cane is then placed to the south, then to the west, and finally to the north. Whereas phase III is expected to strengthen the girl's body, phase V enables her to run fast without getting fatigued.

> After she runs around the cane in the four ways, she will never get tired and will always be able to run fast. Changing Woman gives her power to the girl and this is why it happens this way.
> She runs in the four ways so she will never get tired. Changing Woman ran fast long time ago, they say. That is why the girl runs so fast around (the cane). She wants to be like Changing Woman and run good.

PHASE VI—"CANDY, IT IS POURED" (*kaeni šanałdi*). At the outset of phase VI, the medicine man blesses the pubescent girl by sprinkling a small amount of cattail pollen over her head and shoulders and on the crook of her cane. He then picks up a small basket filled with candy, corn kernels, and (usually) some coins of low denomination. Standing on the buckskin, directly in front of the girl, he pours these contents over her head.

> After he pours it over her head, everything in all the baskets gets holy. Not just the stuff from the basket he pours over her. All the baskets, even the big ones near the buckskin. Because it is holy, all those things, everybody wants it. If you get a piece of candy, you will have plenty food all the time. If you take one of those corns home and plant it, you have plenty corn to bring in later on. You get some money, that means you get rich and never be poor. The girl's power makes all those things holy and good to have.

Following the "pouring of the basket," male relatives of the pubescent girl carry the cartons containing candy and fruit through the crowd, encouraging everyone to reach in and take as much as he can.

PHASE VII—"BLESSING HER" (*banaʔiłdi*). During phase VII, the pubescent girl and her sponsor dance in place, while all adults who so desire line up before the buckskin and repeat for themselves the blessing that inaugurated phase VI. The significance of phase VII is enormous, for anyone who blesses the girl may at the same time request the power of Changing Woman to grant him a personal wish. A few of these are recorded below:

. . . to have a good crop of corn and beans.
. . . to make my sick wife get better.
. . . my cattle, to get fat for sale time.
. . . to cure up my daughter's face. (in reference to a severe case of acne)
. . . rain
. . . my son in Dallas learning to be a barber, not get into any trouble.

PHASE VIII—"THROWING THEM OFF" (*gihiłke*). When phase VIII begins, the pubescent girl steps off the buckskin, picks it up with both hands, shakes it, and then throws it toward the east. Following this, she throws a blanket in each of the three other cardinal directions. According to one informant:

> She does this for two reasons. She throws the blanket so she can always have blankets, plenty of them, in her camp when she gets old. She shakes them out, like if they had dust in them, so her blankets and camp will always be clean. The buckskin she throws so there will always be deermeat in her camp, and good hunting for everyone.

Phase VIII concludes the puberty ceremonial. The girl and her sponsor retire immediately, the crowd disperses, and the medicine man and his drummers leave the danceground in search of shade and something to drink. The sun is now high in the sky; as many as four hours may have elapsed since *nai'es* began.

FOUR "HOLY" DAYS. For four days after *nai'es*, Changing Woman's power continues to reside in the pubescent girl and, acting through her, may be used to cure sickness or bring rain. A medicine man commented:

> At that time she is just like a medicine man, only with that power she is holy. She can make you well if you are sick even with no songs. Anyone who doesn't feel good can come to her, it doesn't matter who it is. Sometimes, if there's been no rain they put that cane in the ground inside (a wickiup or shade) and ask her to sprinkle water on it. That way she can make it rain. I've seen it.

Life-Objectives

The puberty ceremony may be interpreted as isolating symbolically four critical life-objectives towards which all Apache girls on the threshold of adulthood should aspire. These are physical strength, an even temperament, prosperity, and a sound, healthy old age. To understand why these particular life-objectives are emphasized, it will be necessary to consider their relation to other aspects of Western Apache culture:powers; the role of women in the native economy; the conduct of interpersonal relationships; and the natural environment. The significance of achieving life-objectives is apparent only when the consequences and implications of failing to achieve them are understood.

OLD AGE. For the Apache, attaining old age is believed to depend in part upon keeping on good terms with the various powers. As we have seen, these forces continually demand "respect," and failure to observe the taboos surrounding them can lead to sickness and death. A common reaction to the death (by illness) of a young person is "he did something wrong," the implication being that he offended a power and was unable to secure proper treatment. Conversely, the aged are perceived as having consistently avoided situations of this sort; they have maintained amicable relations with the powers and, in so doing, have won out against the vicissitudes of a potentially harmful universe. Unlike ourselves, the Western Apache do not dread old age, they regard it as a positive achievement.

By instructing the pubescent girl how to deal safely with the realm of power, and by stressing the importance of observing taboos, the puberty ceremonial not only defines longevity as a life-objective but also helps the girl attain it. She is provided with a walking cane to use when, as an old woman, she has difficulty getting about. The eagle feather in her hair will cause her to live until she herself turns gray. In phase V of *nai'es* she passes symbolically through the four stages of life. Most important of all, she is invested with the power of Changing Woman, the recognized source and giver of many years. The eagle feathers attached to the girl's cane ward off power-caused illnesses, and the need to observe taboos is emphasized during the ceremony (and for four days following) when the girl is forbidden to scratch herself or drink from a container.

PHYSICAL STRENGTH. Life in Cibecue makes heavy demands on women, and it is essential that they be physically strong. Women do most of the work connected with agriculture: planting; weeding; irrigating; and harvesting. They also attend to a variety of arduous household tasks: preparing food; building wickiups and shades; collecting and chopping firewood; and transporting food and water. Although many families in Cibecue now own trucks or automobiles, it is not at all unusual for a woman to walk over 2 miles from her camp to the trading post and return, often carrying 20 or 30 pounds of groceries. Occasionally, though not nearly as often as in pre-reservation days, women go on long overland treks in search of wild plant foods such as mescal tubers, piñon nuts, and acorns. Hard work is expected of all adult women, and without the physical strength it requires, they place the survival of their families in considerable jeopardy.

A girl's economic education begins in childhood with a few simple domestic chores. At the age of five or six, she may be asked to shuck corn or carry a few empty bottles to the trading post. At ten or eleven, she is given instruction in the techniques of agriculture and food preparation. By the time she reaches adolescence, a girl is thoroughly acquainted with the duties that await her as an adult. The puberty ceremony symbolically awards her the fortitude and endurance she will need to fulfill these duties. In phase III, her body is "molded" to make it strong. By running in the four directions during phase I, she acquires stamina. And throughout the entire ceremony, the eagle feathers on the shoulders of her buckskin sarape invoke a lightness of foot.

AN EVEN TEMPERAMENT. To ready the pubescent girl for life in adult society, *nai'es* confers upon her those qualities considered most necessary for the conduct of successful interpersonal relationships: an even temperament and a good disposition. The value of these qualities is obvious, but they take on particular significance in connection with kinship and belief in witchcraft.

Despite the fact that the economic importance of extended kin groups has waned in recent years, the Apache continues to rely heavily on the members of his matrilineage and clan branch. In the event of serious crisis—lack of food, money, serious illness—these are the people he turns to for support. Put simply, matrilineal kin provide the individual with a safeguard against disaster that he can ill afford to lose, and it is therefore imperative that he take care not to antagonize them. The possibility of falling victim to witchcraft makes offending nonrelatives equally daugerous. (Witchcraft will be discussed in detail in Chapter 6.) Here, we need only note that witches are persons who, when provoked, employ power to harm others, either by causing illness or by destroying livestock and personal property.

Western Apaches value the personality disinclined toward such displays of hostility as might anger a kinsman or upset a potential witch. A highly esteemed person is one who is friendly, generous, and adroit enough to avoid situations which produce interpersonal conflict; he suppresses aggression and is reluctant to pry into other people's affairs. In the puberty ceremonial, these qualities are symbolically bestowed on the pubescent girl by the oriole feathers attached to the eagle feathers on her cane and to her drinking tube; she is ritually awarded those character traits her culture defines as prerequisite for smooth social interaction.

PROSPERITY. In pre-reservation days, prosperity corresponded in large part to the abundance of nature and successful raiding. Today, it means having enough food and money to withstand periods of deprivation. For most Apaches, the business of making a living is difficult and uncertain. Agricultural plots rarely yield heavy crops, and inclement weather sometimes results in no crops at all. For all but a few families, private income is low, and credit at the trading post soon runs out. It is altogether understandable, then, that Apaches think of the prosperous man as one who is free from hunger and want. In phase VI of *nai?es*, the pubescent girl is protected against famine by the corn, candy, and fruit which is cascaded over her head; the buckskin in which she dances throughout the ceremony stands as a guarantee of a plentiful supply of meat.

In recent years, Apaches have come to place a high value on some of the things money can buy. Trucks, for instance, are a welcome means of transportation, opening up wide areas of mobility, and even the simplest cabin provides warmth during the winter. Within the past few decades, the practice of pouring a few coins over the pubescent girl's head has been added to *nai?es*, thus assuring her of wealth as an adult. Older informants point out, however, that in their youth men reckoned wealth in terms of horses, women in terms of blankets. The traditional symbol of wealth, they say, occurs in phase VIII, when the girl throws a blanket in each of the cardinal directions.

Our discussion of life-objectives may have left the impression that Apaches conceive of them as objectively formulated principles. Actually, this is not so; life-objectives are understood implicitly and are rarely verbalized. Their significance lies in the fact that they define patterns of behavior which lessens the hazards and tensions in those areas of life most filled with uncertainty and in which failure may have dire consequences.

Social Functions

Thus far we have been primarily concerned with what the puberty ceremonial does for girls who take part in it. Let us now consider some of the contributions it makes to Apache society at large.

During the days preceding a puberty ceremonial, the obligations which clan and lineage kinship entail are put to a critical test. Without the assistance of kinsmen the ceremony cannot be given. Members of the pubescent girl's clan are expected to contribute large quantities of food and help prepare the danceground. To a lesser extent, relatives of the girl's sponsor are expected to do the same. By stressing the need for close cooperation, ceremonials do much to reinforce clan solidarity. And by demonstrating the practical advantages of extended kinship, they help confirm the utility and effectiveness of the existing social order.

Apaches themselves observe that one of the most important aspects of the puberty ceremonial is the affirmation of the šułke relationship. As previously noted, this institution establishes reciprocal obligations between members of the pubescent girl's family and clan and those of the girl's sponsor. Since obligations of this sort otherwise obtain only between consanguineal kin, the šułke relationship functions to increase significantly the number of people an individual can rely on for support. In effect, šułke makes kinsmen of persons who are totally unrelated.

Anthropologists have noted that one of the primary functions of ritual everywhere is to give systematic protection against the unpredictable, the unforeseen, and the perilous. Malinowski (1931:624) wrote that ritual was "nothing else but an institution which fixes, organizes, and imposes upon the members of a society the positive solution in those inevitable conflicts which arise out of human impotence in dealing with hazardous issues by mere knowledge and technical ability." In providing "solutions," ritual also satisfies the individual's demands for a stable, coercible, and comprehensible world, thereby enabling him to maintain a sense of inner security against the threat of misfortune.

As we have seen, the puberty ceremonial is directed toward those things in life which are essential and therefore desirable. In the face of sickness, hunger, and poverty, it conveys the comforting message that old age, good health, and prosperity are within reach. By suggesting that the "good things" are, in fact, obtainable, nai?es makes the harsh realities of day to day existence seem less threatening and, at least temporarily, easier to contend with. Viewed in this light, female puberty becomes little more than a pretext for invoking the benevolence of Changing Woman's power and bringing the prospect of good fortune to everyone in the community.

Apaches say over and over that everyone "gets something" from nai?es. The corn kernels and money poured over the pubescent girl's head in phase VI allegedly guarantee good crops and wealth; the fruit and candy offer protection against hunger. During phase VII, anyone who wants may request a personal favor of Changing Woman and, for four days after the ceremony, the pubescent girl is "like a medicine man"—she can cure the sick and bring rain. Thus, the puberty ceremonial focuses on problems which are of vital concern to all Apaches and, by holding out the promise of "better times," helps to ease the worry and anxiety that accompanies them.

To the extent that *naiʔes* defines life-objectives as worthy of achievement, it also incites compliance with accepted standards of ethical behavior. Parents, for example, may tell their children: "It is good to have those things they want for that girl when she grows up to be old. All these people will help you if you grow up old that way." And once, after attending a puberty ceremonial, a young man who had lately been in trouble remarked: "I'm going to act good from now on. I sure liked that dance, and I'll try to be like that girl who got that power."

Taken as a whole, the girl's puberty ceremony symbolizes an era of happiness and plenty which, Apaches believe, actually existed in mythological times. "In those days," the people say, "everything was good." The myth of Changing Woman, and her personification by the pubescent girl, link *naiʔes* to the past and thus provide the *raison d'être* for its relevance to the present. Like other Apache rituals, the ultimate justification for *naiʔes* stems not so much from the ceremony itself as from the long cultural tradition of which it is a product.

6

Witchcraft

I N THIS CHAPTER, we will be concerned with a set of beliefs, widely shared among the Western Apache, which imply that certain individuals purposely kill and injure others by means involving neither face-to-face interaction nor the use of any item of material culture. Analogous beliefs have been found to occur in a wide range of human societies, and it has been the general practice for anthropologists to write about them under the heading "witchcraft."

Sorcerers and Love Witches

According to the Apache, there are two types of witch, *iɫkašn* and *odi?i*, which we shall designate, respectively, as "sorcerer" and "love witch." Sorcerers and love witches are distinguished according to differences in the techniques they employ. Love witches make use of *godistso* ("love magic"), which they direct against members of the opposite sex for the purposes of sexual gratification. Sorcerers do not include *godistso* in their repertoire, but resort instead to one or more additional techniques which are said to cause sickness, death, and the destruction of personal property. The several techniques used by sorcerers are labelled by Apache terms which may be glossed as follows: (1) *Poison Sorcery*, which involves the use of a specially prepared "poison," called *iɫkaš*; (2) *Spell Sorcery*, which is essentially enchantment by spell; (3) *Shooting Sorcery*, which entails the injection of a foreign object into the victim's body.

SORCERERS (*iɫkašn*). Sorcerers, Apaches claim, have always been and are today far more numerous than love witches. They are also the most dangerous type of witch. Both men and women become sorcerers, but male sorcerers are said to be more common. This is explained on the grounds that men experience *kedn* ("hatred") more intensely than women. An individual acquires one or all of the techniques of sorcery by learning them from an established practitioner.

73

Sorcerers are reluctant to instruct someone who is not a close maternal kinsman, and the Apache say this results in certain *hati?i* (clan branches) having more sorcerers than others. Persons who wish to learn the techniques of sorcery must pay well for their instruction since experienced sorcerers, kinsmen or not, refuse to part with their knowledge cheaply.

Sorcerers are said to be primarily active at night and are particularly fond of gathering at well-attended ceremonials where their actions will go undetected in the large crowds. The footprints of sorcerers (*iłkašn bi ke*) may be found near burial grounds, or near the wickiups of victims, but they are said to be extremely difficult to identify. If a sorcerer is seen practicing his craft, he should be apprehended and killed on the spot. A captured sorcerer may attempt to buy his freedom with money or livestock, but just as often threatens his captor with sudden death.

POISON SORCERY. Sorcerers are said to carry poison with them at all times, usually in small buckskin pouches hidden beneath their clothing. Poison is commonly administered in food, but it may also be thrown through the door of a wickiup, or simply dropped into the mouth or nostrils of someone asleep.

Of the various sorcery techniques, poison sorcery is the one most often employed against whole groups of people. Strangers who appear unexpectedly and ask to be fed may be carrying poison, and it is expedient to watch them closely, lest they try to deposit it in the cooking pot from which everyone takes his food.

An instance of poison sorcery involving more than one victim is reported in the following account, which deals with a man who traveled to Cibecue from his home in Canyon Day, some 45 miles away.

> X came from Carizzo to be with Y. He said he didn't want anything, come just to visit. Two days went by and nothing happened, but then Y's wife got sick and died. They have for her a wake and bury her. After that Y's little daughter got sick. They (Y and his relatives) got together and said, "I wonder why there is so much sickness just here, nowhere else. Maybe from Carizzo X brought some bad medicine to spread around Cibecue." Then Y went away for one day and came back. Then he said to X, "We can't tell why there is sickness going on just here, nowhere else. It will spread among these poor Apaches. Did you bring poison with you?" Then X said: "No. My relatives are here in Cibecue." But Y's relatives didn't believe what X said and decided to kill him. They went to him again and said, "We think you have poison with you and use it to make these people sick. We might kill you if you don't stop using that poison." Then X said, "Yes, I brought poison and put it all in the food these people have been eating." After that, Y's little girl died and everyone said it was sorcerer from Carizzo made it that way.

SPELL SORCERY. Of the sorcerer's three techniques, spell sorcery is the most varied and complex. Spells may be cast either by uttering a short phrase which promises harm to the intended victim, or more simply, by thinking malicious thoughts about him. In either case, it is not necessary that the sorcerer encounter the person he wishes to harm face-to-face nor, as among the Navaho, to obtain excuvia from him. The phrases used in casting spells may be repeated four times and usually mention the victim's Apache name. They may also include a line from a ceremonial chant said backwards.

A sorcerer may heighten the effectiveness of a spell in any one of the following ways: (1) by walking around the intended victim four times. (This method is said to be most frequently employed at ceremonials); (2) by circling the victim's dwelling four times; (3) by placing four pieces of wood, one at each of the cardinal points, around the victim's wickiup or shack; (4) by burying some object—usually a piece of wood or a small stone—in the ground near the victim's dwelling or at some spot where he habitually goes to drink or relax.

Although spells are directed primarily against human beings, they are also effective against livestock, crops, some items of material culture, and curing ceremonials. When spells are cast on horses and cattle the animals become apathetic and die within a short time. Saddle girths, breast leathers, and bridles are susceptible to spells, and those which break or come loose for no apparent reason may be discarded as having been witched. Most informants maintain that the curative effects of ceremonials can be nullified by spells, but a few said they doubt this is so. A fairly typical example of spell sorcery is described below.

Old X (a medicine man) was singing for Y over at his place one time. I went over there with my cousin. Y was real sick, had a long time hurt in his left arm. X started singing and about half-way through said, "You people here, listen to what I say. Someone has been hurting Y with bad songs. There are some bad songs around here and that is why Y is sick." Then X started to sing again. In the morning, sun came up, X said again, "you people here, listen to me. The person that is trying to hurt this sick man buried something around this place. I think it is in the ground just around here." Then X started to turn over rocks and look under cactus, but he find nothing. Then he walked a little away, those people following him. He came to a big rock where Y used to sit and drink *tułpai.* X looked under the rock and brought out a flat piece of black rock. He said, "here is what his power has been working with. Now that I have found it that person is in for sickness himself, and old Y will get better.

SHOOTING SORCERY. Object intrusion as a form of sorcery is said to have been particularly widespread around 1920 to 1925, when a nativistic movement (compare Goodwin and Kaut 1954) swept across the Fort Apache and San Carlos Reservations. Although most informants maintained it was no longer practiced, all were able to recall stories they had overheard as children about shooting sorcery, and several described concrete instances of it. The projectiles injected by sorcerers —bits of wood, pebbles, beads, arrowheads, strands of hair, and charcoal—travel unerringly over great distances, and are propelled at such high speeds that they become invisible in the air. As illustrated by the following account, a sudden stab of pain tells the victim he has been "hit."

That time I was with X and we were working on the drift fence near that spotted mountain. At night, that time, X was by the fire and eating his grub. He said to me: "I don't feel so good." Then he went to sleep. In the night he woke me up and said: "I was just sleeping there and I wake up with big pain right here, here in my neck. It sure hit me all of a sudden." Then, that time later in the night, it hit him again. He said: "I wonder who is shooting at me." Then I know that someone is after him with shooting sorcery.

LOVE WITCHES (*odi²i*). The use of *godistso* ("love magic") does not necessarily bring about misfortune. It can be used in a diluted or "weak" form (*godistso altsise*) to win friends or attract lovers, and under these conditions is considered neither "bad" (*nčɔ*) nor "dangerous" (*donžoda*). However, when applied to a person in its "strong" form (*godistso nča*)—causing him to experience *nedɯt̜i* ("craziness")—love magic takes on these attributes and becomes a technique of *odi²i*.

Directed against the opposite sex, love magic is said to overcome previous indifference or dislike and create an overwhelming desire to be with the person who has employed it. This soon grows into an uncontrollable obsession, accompanied by heightened sexual desire. Women are said to be more susceptible to love magic than men, and under its influence pursue the love witch wherever he goes and do whatever his wishes.

That time, that big man, they say he did it. Every day he ride his horse up and down the road by X's house. X, she pretend not to notice him but she did. Every day, like that, he ride up and down the road by X's house. Pretty soon X she start to think about that big man, even when he go away, always like that. Then one night at a curing ceremonial she sees him there and go over to where he is standing. But he didn't pay any attention to her. Then he walk away. Next day he ride his horse up and down again, and X she came out to be with him. He took her for a ride, just short way. Then, that time, later on, she have dream about him and want to lie with him. Every time she sees him it was that way for her. She think about it all the time. Then, even in the day, she try to find him, chase him all around these people their camps. Pretty soon she catch him and lie with him. Then they do that for a time. After that that big man want no more of that woman. But she is crazy with that Love Magic and keep after him. She walk all around yelling his name. Pretty soon she says she gonna kill him. That big man hide all this time. Then they have a dance for X and that make her all right. After that she doesn't chase that man anymore.

SORCERER'S SICKNESS (*i̜tkašn kasɯt̜i*). This term is used to describe a variety of symptoms, but all are notable for the fact that they occur without warning and with startling suddenness. This is far and away the most definitive feature of sorcerer's sickness, and the one which is remarked upon most frequently.

The corpses of sorcery victims are said to exhibit swollen tongues and bluish markings around the face and neck. They are also reported to decompose at an unusually rapid rate.

PROTECTION AND CURES. Tangible "protection" (*inkɯzi*) against sorcery is afforded by turquoise beads, cattail pollen, and the breast feathers of eagles. Several informants claimed that the wooden cane used in the girls' puberty ceremonial warded off spells, and one old man said he carried with him at all times a special bean, which would instantly crack open should a sorcerer attempt to harm him.

When an Apache is convinced that he is suffering from sorcerer's sickness, he must choose between two courses of action. He may do nothing, in which case his illness may get worse, or he may seek treatment in the form of a curing ceremonial. Bear ceremonials, snake ceremonials, and lightning ceremonials are performed to combat the work of sorcerers. On rare occasions *gan* ceremonials are held, but for most Apaches the expense of such an undertaking is prohibitive.

In curing ceremonials, the power of the presiding medicine man, aided by appropriate chants, attempts to combat the sorcerer's power. If this is accomplished (and there are times when it is not), the sorcerer will die within a short time and his victim will begin to recover.

TRIALS (*yaiti*). Goodwin (1942:423) reports that if it is considered certain that one person has used witchcraft against another, a close male kinsman of the victim is justified in getting revenge by seeking out the witch and killing him. My informants unanimously disagreed with this, saying that persons accused of sorcery are always given a "trial" (*yaiti*).

According to Goodwin (1942:418) trials follow a definite pattern. They were directed by the headman of a local group, and the suspect was flatly accused of his crime. If he denied it he was strung up by the wrists from the limb of a tree, just high enough that his toes barely touched the ground. Suspects who refused to admit their guilt were left suspended, and fires might be lit beneath them to hasten their confession. They were questioned repeatedly, and their clothes and belongings were searched for poison.

None of my informants admitted to having witnessed a trial, and all stressed that they knew very little about what transpired at such events. They said that only three trials had taken place in the past two decades, and that only one had resulted in the death of a sorcerer.

One man offered a brief description of a contemporary trial. If what he says is true, it is clear that present-day methods for extracting confessions are somewhat less brutal than those employed in pre-reservation times. According to my informant, the suspect is thrust into the center of a large circle of men and is refused food and drink until he confesses. He is warned that if he attempts to escape he will be pursued and shot.

Suspects, Accusations, and "Guilt"

At present, there is no empirical evidence to support the Apaches' contention that human beings actually employ the techniques attributed to sorcerers. Neither the ethnographer, nor his informants, has ever observed a witch in action, watched a witch dance, or seen any of the ritual paraphernalia witches are reported to use. On the other hand, it is an inescapable fact that persons openly declare themselves victims of witchcraft, make accusations, and usually seek some form of ceremonial treatment. Many adult Apaches carry protection against sorcery. Sorcerer's sickness is recognized as an appropriate diagnosis for certain kinds of symptoms, and medicine men proficient at curing them are highly esteemed.

It is possible that some Western Apaches do not believe unequivocally in the validity of witchcraft. Statements of the following sort are not uncommon: "I could tell you all those things I have heard about witches, but I don't think they are true," or "Maybe there were witches long ago when those old people had strong power, but I don't think they can hurt you with it anymore." During the initial stages of my fieldwork I accepted these and similar remarks at face value, but when one of my most skeptical acquaintances attributed the death of an infant girl to poison sorcery it became apparent that in times of crises early conditioning was liable to prevail. This impression was repeatedly confirmed. Although the possibility cannot be ruled out that some individuals genuinely doubt the existence of witches, the vast majority of Apaches in Cibecue behave in ways which make sense—to one another as well as to the observer—only on the assumption that their belief in witchcraft is widely shared.

WITCH SUSPECTS. How are specific individuals identified as witch suspects or, more simply, on what basis do the Apache make accusations?

Although students of witchcraft in other societies have devoted relatively little attention to this problem, a moment's reflecion will show that it is of critical importance. For unless it can be demonstrated that decisions about who is a suspect and who is not are made according to definite criteria, we have no alternative but to assume that witches are accused at random; namely, that anyone, at any place, at any time, and for whatever reason has just as much chance of being accused as anyone else. With respect to the Western Apache such an assumption proves untenable. Apaches make accusations only when they perceive that the behavior of a given individual—the accused witch—exhibits a set of specific attributes. These are the criteria which serve to distinguish suspects from nonsuspects and, as such, make the accusation of witches anything but haphazard.

Suppose we wish to write a set of rules that would allow us to distinguish members of the Apache botanical category *hwoš* from members of other botanical categories. This will be a relatively easy task because we will soon discover that *hwoš* correctly labels only those flora which have thorns. With no more information that this we can assign each plant we see to the *hwoš* category (if it has thorns) or to some other (if it does not). The point to be stressed is this: members of the category *hwoš* can be unequivocally identified because their defining attribute is readily observable and verifiable. In comparison, members of the category *iłkašn* (sorcerer) cannot be unequivocally identified because their defining attribute is *not* observable. Human beings are never observed practicing witchcraft, and there is no way of proving that they have. Consequently, it is impossible to know for certain that someone is a witch.

Because accusations cannot proceed from the empirical fact of witchcraft, they can only be based on the grounds that behavior of particular individuals conforms to culturally defined criteria for *suspicion* of witchcraft. To the Apache the question: "What must I know to prove that someone is a witch?" is irrelevant, for proof in the realm of witchcraft is simply not possible. The relevant question is "What must I know to suspect that someone is a witch?" Since the ethnographer —like his informants—is unable to specify criteria that distinguish witches from nonwitches, the best he can do is to specify those that distinguish suspects from nonsuspects.

Knowledge of the criteria for suspicion of witchcraft is essential in evaluating the plausibility of accusations. (The *validity* of an accusation is never in question because guilt can never be proven or disproven.) An accusation will be considered plausible when the actions of a person accused are judged to satisfy the criteria for suspicion. It will be considered implausible when the accused's behavior is interpreted as not satisfying the suspicion criteria. The "guilt" of an Apache accused of witchcraft is thus determined by the degree to which other Apaches consider his accusation plausible. It should be noted, however, that some of the suspicion criteria are extremely vague and, as such, open to a wide variety of interpretations. This causes the Apache to disagree about the plausibility of accusations and, by the same token, about the guilt of accused witches.

The criteria for suspicion of witchcraft fall into two sets. The first, which we shall label *nonbehavioral*, refers to features of a person's status, both ascribed and achieved. The second set consists of *behavioral* criteria; these refer to the psychological condition of individuals and to their overt actions, their observable behavior.

The nonbehavioral attributes of witch suspects as given by Apaches are the following: (1) *nde diyin bił*, or *diyin* ("persons with power"); (2) *dohwakida* ("persons who do not belong to one's own phratry"); (3) *nde mbaiyən* ("persons at or beyond the age-stage *mbaiyən*").

PERSONS WITH POWER. A prerequisite for the practice of witchcraft is the possession of a power. Conversely, individuals who are thought to lack a power are automatically ruled out. For an Apache ill with sorcerer's sickness this means that in addition to medicine men, anyone he thinks might be shielding a secret power qualifies as a legitimate suspect.

The Apache emphasize that, medicine men aside, it may be difficult to tell who possesses power and who does not. Several informants said that "rich people" (*nde izisnetıni*) could generally be counted on to have it, as could individuals who had lived for a long time without getting seriously ill. However, several other informants maintained that these criteria were not always applicable or sufficient. Considerable ambiguity surrounds the concept of power, and the question of whether or not a person possesses it frequently emerges as a focal point of contention in the disputes which follow upon accusations.

PERSONS WHO DO NOT BELONG TO ONE'S OWN PHRATRY. One of the most explicit criteria for distinguishing witch suspects from nonsuspects is that the former cannot be Ego's *ki ąłhanigo* ("members of Ego's clan") or *ki* ("members of clans related to Ego's"). Theoretically, Ego is immune to witchcraft practiced by persons belonging to his own phratry. The only people who can witch him are *dohwakida*; that is, members of his father's clan (*banestį*), members of his spouse's clan (*šaʔadni*), and members of all other clans unrelated to his own (*dohandago*).

The Apache offer two explanations as to why this is so. The first and most common is that a man's power will have no effect on someone who belongs to his own phratry since they are both "of the same blood;" instead, it will ricochet off the intended victim and return to strike dead the person who employed it. The second explanation is that although phratry members frequently behave badly toward each other they do not seek revenge by resorting to witchcraft. Tactics of this sort are used only by *dohwakida*. Regardless, it is a notable fact that of the twenty-seven cases of witchcraft recorded in Cibecue since 1960, only one involved the accusation of a phratry member. More important, the man accused in this instance was immediately vindicated on the grounds that he *was* of a clan related to that of the accuser and, as such, could not be guilty of the charge.

PERSONS AT OR BEYOND THE AGE-STAGE (*mbaiyən*). This criterion is grounded in the assumption that the practice of witchcraft in all its forms calls for "strong power" (*diyi ṅčahi*), and that power is strongest when employed by someone who is *mbaiyən* or older. Prior to this it is too "weak" (*altsise*) for witchcraft. The *mbaiyən* age-stage criterion effectively disqualifies younger Apaches as witch suspects. Of all the accused witches in our twenty-seven case sample, only one was under forty years of age.

The nonbehavioral attributes discussed above define a broad category of persons "capable" of practicing witchcraft against a particular Ego. As such, they serve to delimit significantly the field of possible suspects (see Figure 11). However, in and out of themselves they do not constitute sufficient grounds for accusing a particular individual. In addition to exhibiting nonbehavioral attributes a witch suspect must also meet behavioral criteria. And to these we now turn.

The behavioral attributes of witch suspects must be understood in relation to the Apaches conviction that *kedn* ("hatred") is what motivates people to learn and employ the techniques of witchcraft. If there were no *kedn*, my informants said, there would be no sorcerer's sickness, no love sickness, and no accusations. In short, there would be no witches.

The appropriate behavioral criteria for identifying a witch suspect are those which enable an Apache to decide whether or not someone hates him. These are the following:

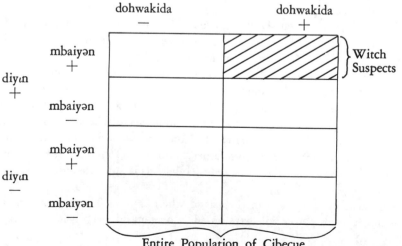

Entire Population of Cibecue

Key:

dohwakida —:	members of own phratry
dohwakida +:	members of other phratries
mbaiyən —:	persons below age-stage *mbaiyən*
mbaiyən +:	persons at or beyond age-stage *mbaiyən*
diyın —:	persons not possessing power
diyın +:	persons possessing power

(1) *niʔai čįʔį* ("he is stingy to you")

(2) *nina dagodnɬtahi* ("he starts fights with you")

(3) *niʔhaškeʔ* ("he is angry with you")

(4) *niʔnaškeʔ* ("he is mean to you")

(5) *nɬiʔ iɬcǫʔi* ("he lies about you")

(6) *niʔa ɬagoʔahi* ("he tells stories about you")

(7) *niʔa nagoʔahi* ("he makes threats to you")

(8) *ni čındi ndihi* ("he informs on you")

(9) *niʔa netıni* ("he makes fun of you")

(10) *niʔadt bananda* ("he propositions your wife")

(11) *niʔadt nantį nanda* ("he fornicates with your wife")

(12) *niʔın* ("he steals from you")

(13) *haɬ niʔ haɬloʔ nikedn di hiwa* ("he got into trouble with you before and hates you because of it")

Figure 11. Witch suspects defined on basis of nonbehavioral attributes.

Criteria 10, 11, and 12 are self-explanatory, but the others call for brief comment.

1. *niʔai čįʔį* ("he is stingy to you"). The Apache usually request large favors only in times of crisis, and this criterion refers most specifically to the refusal of money, goods, or physical labor when they are needed to meet an emergency.

2. *nina dagodnɬtahi* ("he tries to start fights with you"). This phrase describes persons who start fights and quarrels without provocation; that is, for no apparent reason other than their own desire to get embroiled and, should they emerge victorious, to discredit their opponent.

3 and 4. *niʔhaškeʔ* ("he is angry with you") and *niʔnaškeʔ* ("he is mean to you"). Criteria 3 and 4 are best considered in relation to one another. The term *haškeʔ* describes a quickness to anger and a willingness to express it openly and directly, apparently without fear of recrimination; *naškeʔ* refers to the same basic ill temper but with the difference that it is kept hidden or revealed in petty, nonobvious ways.

5 and 6. *nɬiʔ iɬcǫʔi* ("he lies about you"), *niʔa ɬagoʔahi* ("he tells stories about you"). To the Apache, "lying" and "telling stories" are two different things. The former consists of taking an acknowledged fact or an actual event and distorting it far out of all proportion. The latter involves the voicing of deliberate falsehoods, which have no basis in fact and are solely the product of someone's imagina-

tion. Both share the attribute of being prompted by malice, and both are designed to reflect badly on the persons to whom they pertain.

7. *niʔa nagoʔahi* ("he makes threats to you"). The gloss "threatens" must be understood here in an unusually broad sense, for to an Apache, *nago* can refer not only to statements which promise harm (for example, "I will kill you") or the destruction of personal property (for example, "I will burn your corn"), but also to any suggestion that misfortune is imminent (for example, "Your baby could die if you don't get it cured" or "Your corn could rot if you don't give some of it away."). Generally speaking, the Apache are very reluctant to give advice, and a primary reason is that unless one is careful, "advice" may be construed as a threat.

8. *ni čındi ndihi* ("he informs on you"). In the case of minor offenses, such as "drunk in public" and "disturbing the peace," an Apache policeman cannot make a legal arrest until someone registers a verbal complaint against the offender. Since most Apaches strongly prefer to settle their differences out of court, there is considerable pressure not to file complaints. Persons who do are held directly responsible for any arrests that follow and are apt to become bitter enemies. They are the informers to which this criterion refers.

9. *niʔa netıni* ("he makes fun of you"). Apaches who get on well with one another joke constantly. Usually, jokes take the form of back-handed compliments, that is, outwardly critical remarks which are intended to indicate that what is denounced is actually held in high esteem (for example, one man to another, concerning the latter's daughter who is widely admired for her comely appearance and industriousness: "You must be afraid of that girl. You should tell that ugly child of yours not to be so lazy."). Occasionally, people who dislike each other will pretend to joke, but in this case no compliments are exchanged, criticism is real, and the person at whom the joke is directed is made to feel stupid, imprudent, or inept. This is what the Apache has in mind when he speaks of people "making fun" of him.

13. *hał niʔ hałloʔ nikedn di hiwa* ("he got into trouble with you before and hates you because of it"). The Apache believe firmly that participants in violent quarrels or fights continue to resent each other for a long time thereafter and, to make matters worse, constantly search for opportunities to get revenge. It is frequently said: "These Apaches around here never forget who fights them." In view of this attitude, it is not surprising that persons with whom one has experienced open conflict in the past, rate as primary witch suspects. Of the twenty-seven accusations we recorded, all but eight involved persons who had previously engaged in fights and/or public altercations.

Taken singly, the various criteria for suspicion of witchcraft appear quite indefinite. Collectively, however, they serve to define a fairly specific "type-individual:" an older person (age-stage *mbaiyən*), of a clan unrelated to Ego's, who possesses power and who behaves (or has behaved) toward Ego in ways indicative of hatred. In a community as small as Cibecue, not many people will qualify on all these counts, and as a consequence the number of persons a given Ego can plausibly accuse is sharply limited. Nevertheless, owing to the wide range of interpretation which some of the suspicion criteria admit, accusations are frequently accompanied by disagreement and dispute.

ACCUSATIONS AND DISPUTES. Persons suspected of practicing witchcraft are openly accused by the victim and (usually) the members of his immediate family. When word reaches the alleged witch he is faced with an important decision. He can either feign complete ignorance of the charge—an act which may be interpreted by his accusers as a sign of guilt—or he can openly contest the accusation and attempt to convince his accusers that he has been falsely maligned.

It is said that an accused witch will remain silent only when he cannot refute the charges leveled against him or, in our terms, when he is unable to adduce evidence which effectively demonstrates that he does not exhibit the attributes of a witch suspect. In such a case his accusation will be considered plausible by other people, public opinion will be on the side of the accuser, and protestations of innocence—if the suspect makes them—will be of no avail. The Apache insist that refusal to dispute an accusation does not prove unequivocally that the subject is a witch, but it is my impression that they regard it as coming closer to an admission of guilt than anything else.

The case described below gives an example of an accusation that went undisputed.

Case Number 1. On August 17, 1966, X came down with severe pains at the base of his spine. Two days later the illness was diagnosed as a case of shooting sorcery, and X accused Y of practicing witchcraft. Y was a man about 50 years old (*mbaiyən*), and belonged to a clan, *dušdoę*, which was unrelated to X's (*iyaʔaiye*). In support of his accusation X offered the following reasons:

1. Y had a power. As a young man he had openly declared that he could use it to find lost objects, and on many occasions he had boasted of how it had told him when to buy horses and pick-up trucks. He also claimed it helped him win at gambling.

2. Y had "shown hatred" toward X. One night, when drunk, he accused X of stealing a saddle. He had also refused to give X apples when the latter was out of work, and his family needed food. At a recent ceremonial he had propositioned X's wife. And, on several occasions, he had exaggerated the facts surrounding an incident when X was thrown from his horse in such a way as to portray X as an incompetent rider.

Everyone with whom I spoke after the accusation—twenty-three men and nine women—agree that Y had done all the things X said and, as such, the accusation appeared plausible. Y did not dispute the accusation.

In disputing an accusation there are two basic strategies (frequently employed simultaneously) with which an alleged witch can attempt to convince his accuser and the community at large that he is innocent. He can demonstrate either that the accuser's charges have no basis in fact, or that they are based on events which have been overly magnified in importance and subsequently misinterpreted. The following account gives some idea of the grounds on which accusations are disputed, and how an alleged witch goes about defending himself.

Case Number 2. On the morning of May 29, 1962, X took to his bed with severe abdominal pains which continued intermittently throughout the day.

On the following morning he felt better, but by noon the cramps had returned. That evening, in the company of his wife and two elder brothers, X announced that he was a victim of poison sorcery, and that Y was responsible. Y was about 55 years of age (*mbaiyən*) and of a clan (*čičisčine*) unrelated to X's (*dziɬtadn*). X used the following reasons to support his charge:

1. Y had a power. On more than one occasion, X had detected a willingness on Y's part to sing at ceremonials, particularly chants from the Bear corpus. Y was wealthy with a steady job and a sizeable cattle herd which increased yearly. He often boasted about not being seriously ill, and had once been heard to say that this was because "something was looking out for him."

2. Y had "shown hatred" toward X. He had refused X money when the latter needed it for a curing ceremony, and years before had been unwilling to sell X a small cornfield. More recently, he had accused X in public of being lazy.

On June 1, two days after the accusation, Y informed several of his close kinsmen that the charges were untrue. He defended his position by pointing out that he had never claimed to have a power and did not have it. He sang enthusiastically at ceremonials only because he liked to sing. True, he was relatively well off, but this was because he had inherited cattle from a deceased maternal uncle and worked hard. He was rich because he was industrious, not because he had power. He was pleased to enjoy good health, but his remark about being "looked out for" (which he could not remember making) was certainly not intended to imply that he was under the protection of a power.

Y said further that the reason he had refused X money for the curing ceremonial was because his sister was ill at the time, and he felt obliged to give her whatever money he could spare. He did not sell X the cornfield because he wanted to save it for his daughter when she married. It was true, however, that he had said X was lazy. This he could not dispute.

When word of Y's defense had circulated, it became apparent that most of the people in Cibecue (except X and the members of his family) considered the accusation implausible. Y said no more. For a few days X insisted that people had "closed their ears too soon," but a month later he admitted that Y might not have been responsible after all.

In the disputes that accompany witchcraft accusations, controversy most often centers on (1) whether the alleged witch possesses a power; and/or (2) whether his behavior towards the accuser can be explained on grounds other than hatred. The Apache admit that these concepts are difficult to define precisely, and they are not at all surprised that, except when confronted with unambiguous evidence such as someone saying "I hate him" or "I have a power," different individuals disagree as to when they are applicable. Actions and utterances which one man judges to be motivated by hatred can be interpreted very differently by another, and (except in the case of medicine men) the same is true of behavior related to the possession of a power. This is why disputes can and do arise, and why opinions concerning the guilt of a witch suspect are sometimes diametrically opposed.

"GUILT" AND ITS CONSEQUENCES. So far as I know, instances of witchcraft are never brought to the attention of white law-enforcement officials and as a result never reach the Tribal Court in Whiteriver. Although Indian police frequently learn of accusations, they are reluctant to report them for the following reasons: First, witchcraft is an offense that white men do not recognize or understand and, even if they did, would probably dismiss it as being devoid of tangible grounds for arrest. Second, any Apache policeman who reported an accusation would be regarded by the persons involved as an informer—a charge to be avoided if at all possible. In short, witchcraft is kept effectively outside the jurisdiction of Western law and, as such, remains one of the few types of offense that the Apache handle completely by themselves.

Although no formal sentences are imposed, it is quite evident that witch suspects who have been accused on numerous occasions, and who have refused to dispute or failed repeatedly in the attempt, are held to be irrevocably guilty. Public opinion becomes so firmly fixed against these individuals that they can do nothing to change it. In future accusations the possibility of their innocence will be ruled out a priori, and no amount of protest, however plausible, can succeed in establishing it. As one informant put it:

> Our ears are closed to those witches and nothing they can do will open them. They have done it too much and can't get out of it. They can try to lie about it if they want, but we still know they did it.

On the other hand, suspects who have disputed their accusations successfully are assumed to be innocent, and in the event of a subsequent accusation will be able to dispute the charges in an atmosphere where their guilt is an open question and not a foregone conclusion. So long as an Apache is able to refute accusations of witchcraft convincingly, he will not encounter serious difficulty. He will be criticized, cautioned by his relatives to be more careful about how he behaves, and in all likelihood his relations with his accuser will be strained for years to come. But in the eyes of most people he will be regarded as someone who was accused through no real fault of his own, and the pattern of his life will not be dangerously disrupted or significantly altered. Still, a precedent has been set, and the suspect knows that if he is accused again public support might be harder to win. On the other hand, someone who consistently elects not to contest accusations, or who is unable to refute them, can become the object of harsh discrimination. He will be spoken of as "heavy with hatred" (*kedn ndaz*), as a potential source of illness, and as someone to be both feared and avoided. Under these circumstances far-reaching changes are bound to occur in his relationships with other people. The most obvious would appear to be the weakening and/or severing of reciprocal obligations with clan and phratry kinsmen, but as the following accounts so plainly illustrate, the denial of critical rights and duties may also be involved.

The first account deals with a man, X, who has been accused three times and who was unable to dispute on each occasion. The second concerns a woman, Y, who was accused twice but, like X, did not dispute. The third account pertains to Z, a medicine man, who has been the object of at least three accusations. He attempted to refute all three, but was successful only once.

They know it, the people living here, that X is a witch. He never said he didn't use it. I guess that's why. All the time, that man get into trouble, and these people here in Cibecue know he hates them. That is why he has lost his friends, and these people here stay away from him. Even his clan (relatives). One time I was at X's cousin's camp and he walked into it. He said it to her, his cousin: "My cousin, give me some money. I need it for drinking." She didn't say anything so he said it again: "I need money. Give it to me. Nobody will help me out." Then she said: "Nobody will help you out because you do bad things and make people sick. If I give you money for drinking, you will get twisted around yourself and start to threaten people again. Go away. I don't want any trouble from someone who does those bad things."

Before these people knew he was a witch, X had many friends but he lost them. I was there at his brother's camp when he walked in. "My brother," he said, "I want to use your truck to go to Showlow to buy groceries." His brother got mad. "You are not my brother. We try to help people around here, but you must make them sick. That is what these people say. Go away."

When X was young, that old man taught him how to make *gan* masks. X sure learned how to do it good. But now they don't want him to help, maybe because he will put bad power on them. He goes around saying that the *gan* masks are no good and fall apart. But even that old man who taught him doesn't want him to do it.

That old woman, Y, she does it. Her father did it too, they say. All these people here know that. They don't want her around, and that's why she lives up there at "running water crosses the trail" (a spot some 3 miles north of Cibecue proper). Before they knew about it, she was pretty rich, but people don't want to help her anymore. She is poor now, and angry with hatred at everybody.

Last year, at the time to pick up acorns, some women of her clan were going out to get some. Y went down to where they were getting ready and said it: "You women, hear what I say. Let me go to where you are going with you to pick up acorns." Then when one woman said it: "I am not of your clan and you might get angry and make me sick. You have done it before. Let us go alone, or I will stay behind."

Over there, across the creek, Y's brother has a big cornfield. He used to let Y use it to farm. But one time when she wanted to plant it he said to her: "When you were not full of hatred for people I let you use my field, but I don't want these people here in Cibecue to think you're too friendly with me. They may think you will teach me how to do it. There is good dirt where you live. Make a farm up there.

It has always been that way with Y. But before they knew it about her, these people in Cibecue, her mother's sister said that when her body was buried she would leave Y a farm. Then Y witched a woman. After that the people got afraid of her. When her aunt died she didn't give anything to Y. She didn't want to give anything to a witch, even though they were close relatives.

After these people knew it about Z they got afraid of him. Before he was pretty good medicine man, but after he did it none of these people used him any more. So he didn't sing anymore at ceremonials and got poor.

One time that man, A, his baby got sick. Z heard about it and walked over to that man's camp. He said it: "I hear your baby is sick. I will sing for that baby." Then A thought about it and said: "We don't know how you use your power. These people say you use it the wrong way. The words (that is, gossip) say you make people sick with it so you can sing for them and get their money." Then Z said: "These people always lie about me; what they say is lies." Then that man A said it: "I don't know what they say if it is lies. But we don't want you to sing here. You might want to make someone sick." So Z walked out of that camp.

In extreme cases, the consequences of being a guilty witch can result in almost complete social ostracism. Two of the individuals mentioned above now live in virtual isolation several miles from the main settlement of Cibecue. They come to the trading post only when they need groceries and rarely attend social and ceremonial events. Said one informant, "Nobody wants them and that is why they stay away."

The Gains and Costs of Witchcraft

In assessing the various functions of witchcraft, we shall accept Kluckhohn's basic postulate that

> . . . no cultural forms survive unless they constitute responses which are adjustive or adaptive, in some sense, for the members of the society or for the society considered as a unit. "Adaptive" is a purely descriptive term referring to the fact that certain types of behavior result in survival (for the individual or for the society as a whole). "Adjustive" refers to those responses which bring about an adjustment in the individual. . . . (Kluckhohn 1944:46).

Among the Western Apache one of the most obvious ways in which belief in witchcraft functions adjustively is by supplying answers to anxiety-provoking problems which might otherwise be difficult to explain. As a legitimate diagnostic category, sorcerer's sickness accounts for sudden illness without apparent etiology, death without visible cause, and several of the diseases which kill and weaken livestock. By the same token, love sickness provides a reason for aberrant behavior perceived to be motivated by uncontrolled sexual desire. The availability of witchcraft as an explanation also contributes to the Apaches' conviction in the validity of their ceremonials. Sometimes even the most carefully performed rituals are unsuccessful in producing cures, but since these failures can be attributed to forces extrinsic to the ceremonials themselves—sorcerer's spells—belief in the effectiveness of ritual is sustained.

Persons suspected of witchcraft are by definition guilty of hatred, and I am convinced that in making accusations most Western Apache feel they are taking tangible steps to get back at someone whom they resent and who, in their opinion, has treated them unfairly. By venting hostility in the form of an accusation rather than, let us say, direct physical attack, the accuser derives certain advantages. First of all, he is able to present an image of himself as a helpless innocent, as one who has been victimized without provocation by a cruel and powerful adversary. In this way, his own animosities remain concealed, whereas those of the alleged witch (which may be real or imagined) are exposed and publicized. Also, the accuser is aware that if the suspect cannot refute the accusation he will suffer unpleasant consequences. If the matter is pursued no further, witchcraft accusations are seen to function adjustively by providing the individual with an outlet for the covert release of aggression, notably one which results in a minimum of punishment for the aggressor.

It should be noted, however, that under certain circumstances the adjustive rewards thus acquired are highly temporary. It sometimes happens that a victim of witchcraft makes an accusation and then, on second thought, wishes he had not. "Could I have accused the wrong person?" "Will that man I said did it try to get after me?" "Maybe I should have waited a little longer." Misgivings of this sort can be every bit as productive of anxiety as the conditions which originally prompted the accusation, and perhaps even more so, since once the accusation has been made the witchcraft victim has no one to blame for his troubles except himself. Should the pressure become too intense, and especially if it is also felt by the victim's close kin, relief may be obtained simply by retracting the accusation. This happens only rarely (twice in the twenty-seven cases on record), but it serves to point up the fact that the act of accusing a witch may be a source of anxiety in and of itself, and that withdrawing accusations sometimes constitutes just as much of an adjustive response as making them.

The absence of matrilineal relationships between alleged witches and their accusers suggests that belief in witchcraft may be instrumental in directing aggression outside Ego's kin group and, to the degree that this helps preserve internal solidarity, functions adaptively. If I have given the impression that clan and phratry groupings in Western Apache society represent paragons of harmonious interaction, some corrections are definitely in order. Tensions do arise and not infrequently. Fights occur, and gossip is filled with complaints about the shortcomings of maternal relatives: how they refuse to help when needed most, or make unreasonable demands, or get abusive when drunk. It is altogether likely, therefore, that the aggressions which motivate witchcraft accusations are regularly compounded by frustrations generated by intrakin group conflict. The important thing of course, is that in spite of this, matrilineal kin are hardly ever formally accused.

The fact that witch suspects are partially defined by their status as *dohwakida* does much to strengthen the Apaches' belief that nonphratry members, no matter how friendly they may seem, are likely to be deceitful and antagonistic. A standard characterization of *dohwakida* is that they are "foxy" or "like coyotes," epithets which underscore their reputed predilection for devious and unpredictable behavior. The knowledge that a witch's power is ineffective against phratry members removes an element of fear from matrilineal relationships, and it could be argued that this, too, contributes positively to the maintenance of kin group cohesiveness. However, as the following example shows, by predisposing the Apache to suspect the motives and intentions of persons belonging to phratries other than his own, belief in witchcraft can also impair interkin group cooperation.

A few years ago, Bureau of Indian Affairs officials at Whiteriver obtained funds to install a modern plumbing system at Cibecue. Labor for the project, which consisted mainly of digging trenches and laying pipe, was to be supplied by the

Apache, and all adult males in Cibecue who were not already employed were asked to participate. On the first day of work a group of thirty-one men turned out: seventeen belonged to phratry 3; eleven to phratry 1; and two to phratry 2 (see Table 3). At the outset work went well, but on the third day the two members of phratry 2 informed a white supervisor they were quitting. A short time later a member of phratry 1 requested that he and his relatives be given a job away from the main body of workmen. A suitable task was found, and the members of phratry 1 separated from the members of phratry 3. Thereafter, the supervisor was unable to re-unite them. The reason for the split, according to my informants, was that two of the men in phratry 3 were known to have power and had a reputation for angering easily; one had previously been accused of witchcraft. Several of the men in phratry 1 were reluctant to work with them because of this, and persuaded their fellows that it was desirable for all concerned to keep the groups apart.

It would be a serious mistake to infer from this one case that the members of different phratries consistently refuse to participate with one another in collective activities; numerous examples to the contrary could be cited. The plumbing incident simply illustrates the Apache's desire to minimize contact with persons he perceives to exhibit the attributes of a witch suspect. This creates relatively few problems, however, because most of the time such individuals can be avoided fairly easily. It is only on those occasions where avoidance is difficult or impossible —where the individual is in some sense *forced* to interact with someone he considers a potential suspect—that the threat of witchcraft hampers cooperation and interferes with interphratry activities.

An accusation of witchcraft is a serious indictment, for it asserts that one man has acted out of "hatred" toward another and has deliberately attempted to harm him. Even if an alleged witch is able to refute his accusation he will be sharply criticized and urged to alter his ways. If the accusation cannot be refuted he is faced with the possibility of rejection by his kinsmen and, in extreme cases, almost total ostracism. As an implied threat, the consequences of being accused of witchcraft discourage behavior which generates or intensifies conflict and, in so doing, emphasizes the advantages of maintaining amicable social relations.

In rationalizing the value of normative behavior to older children, Apaches are apt to explain that one very good reason for being generous, helpful, and paying strict attention to the obligations one has to others is that individuals who are lax in these matters regularly "do bad things," "get into trouble," and "get people mad at them." In context remarks of this sort refer unmistakably to witchcraft. Thus, as a fear-inducing mechanism, operative in advanced stages of the enculturation process, witchcraft may be said to perform an adaptive function by encouraging adherence to existing norms. The following example illustrates this point rather clearly.

> I have heard about what you did at X's place. The men over there gave you cold beer and you got twisted around yourself. Then you got X's son mad at you and made him fight. It is bad what you did. These people around here in your camps don't like it what you did. They are afraid you will stay in trouble with people all the time. Act like you should. Now I will say it, my son. You

are just a boy, but you should know it is bad to make people hate you like that. If you keep doing that someone may try to make you sick, use some of it (power) on you.

It may also be the case that love witchcraft, which is associated with overly familiar behavior toward consanguineal relatives of the opposite sex, serves as a pretext for sanctioning liaisons prohibited by the rules of clan exogamy. On several occasions I have heard stories about young men striking up friendships with girls whose clans were related to their own. Adults, taking note of the situation (and perhaps fearing that it might ultimately lead to sexual relations), expressed their disapproval by saying that such behavior was characteristic of *odiʔi* ("love witches").

Fear of being accused of witchcraft is one of several factors which operate to discourage the accumulation of wealth. If the wealthy refuse to share their surplus goods or funds with others, it is almost certain that word of their stinginess—a prominent attribute of witch suspects—will start to circulate. Prompted by a wish to avoid criticism and suspicion, they may decide to bestow small gifts upon the less fortunate, sponsor drinking parties, and attempt to make it known generally that in times of need their assistance can be counted upon. I should confess that my data on this point are somewhat sparse; in fact, I recorded only six instances in which an individual freely admitted that fear of suspicion of witchcraft motivated him to give away money or material possessions. However, I was led to believe by my informants that this happened quite often. Their statements (which I have no reason to doubt), together with my own observations, suggest the possibility that insofar as it inhibits the stock-piling of wealth, witchcraft functions adaptively by making some of the economic resources of the rich available to the poor.

Witchcraft can also be instrumental in keeping medicine men from becoming too powerful. A medicine man who charges exorbitant fees, who consistently fails to effect cures, or who insists that his patients undergo repeated ceremonial treatment, may be suspected of causing sickness in order to be paid for curing it. When this happens his services will no longer be sought and, if chanting is his only means of support, he may be reduced to poverty within a few months.

For the simple reason that acts of aggression typically associated with witch suspects are also those which antagonize witches and prompt them to get revenge through the use of power, the fear of falling victim to witchcraft, like the fear of being accused, motivates the Apache to mask signs of animosity. As noted earlier, this is particularly true in the presence of older persons with power and medicine men. To refuse the wishes of the aged is to run a serious risk, and one of the most striking adaptive functions of belief in witchcraft is the role it plays in contributing to their physical welfare. Elderly nonkinsmen, some of whom are quite unable to fare for themselves, are regularly given food, shelter, and transportation. No doubt this is sometimes prompted by a genuine desire to be helpful, but it is frequently explained on the grounds that to do otherwise would be to invite retaliation in the form of "sorcerer's sickness."

Finally, as the following incident indicates, the persistence of witchcraft beliefs may function as a brake against the forces of culture change. Several years ago, agency officials at Whiteriver inaugurated a program aimed at increasing the amount of water available for irrigation purposes. In the community of Cibecue, this involved cutting down a number of large cottonwood trees along Cibecue Creek. Most of the Apaches in Cibecue did not understand the ultimate objective of the agency's actions, and were deeply disturbed by what appeared to them the wanton destruction of a valuable natural resource. Before long, people began to remind each other that the two Apaches hired to fell the trees had both been previously accused of witchcraft. Although they had refuted their accusations successfully, and had not been accused a second time, their willingness to "kill cottonwoods" in the face of unanimous public disapproval suggested that they might not be as innocent as had formerly been supposed. This idea was repeated in gossip and quickly gained currency. Within a few days, the tree-cutters quit their jobs.

7

Missionaries

The Early Years

CHRISTIAN MISSIONARIES have been present on what is now the Fort Apache Indian Reservation for well over sixty years. Following on the heels of the U.S. Cavalry, they came on foot and by wagon and built missions of sun-baked adobe. At these tiny outposts, they planted gardens, raised the cross, and started to preach the gospel. The pagan population they sought to convert was anything but receptive. Still recovering from the shock of defeat and subjugation, and trying to adjust to the exigencies of reservation life, the Western Apache were far more concerned with survival than salvation. The missionaries experienced little active resistance, but neither did they make much progress. For the most part, it appears, the Apache simply ignored them.

In response to the anxieties and tensions created by a new and unsatisfactory style of living, the native ceremonial system flourished vigorously. In 1904, a visitor to Fort Apache reported: "There was a ceremony almost every night. Somewhere drums are always to be heard." The years after 1910 were marked by the emergence of several extremely influential medicine men, among them one Silas John who, in 1924 and 1925, headed a small-scale nativistic movement aimed at restoring the conditions of aboriginal life and ridding Fort Apache of an increasing number of witches (Kaut and Goodwin 1954; Basso 1969). Although the symbolism and ideology of American Indian nativism typically combines Christian elements with those from the indigenous culture, no such synthesis appears to have characterized the movement headed by Silas John.[1] Judging from the only published account of the movement, it was in all essential respects strictly Apachean. This is a tenuous bit of evidence on which to base judgment, but it seems reasonable to suppose that, as late as the mid-twenties, Christian influence on the Western Apache belief system was negligible.

[1] Information secured after this manuscript went to press indicates that the movement headed by Silas John was considerably more synthetic—and therefore typical of American Indian nativistic cults—than this statement would suggest.

In any event, the missionaries stayed on. And when the turbulence of the early reservation years had died down, their numbers increased. Adobe missions were replaced by churches of wood and stone, and interpreters were found to translate the words of God. Schools were built to give Apache children instruction in the Bible and, from time to time, food, clothing, and medicines were given away. All the while, the missionaries preached. Extolling the benefits of Christianity, they condemned with equal conviction the evils of the "Apache way." Much of their criticism was directed against medicine men, whom one missionary described as "dogs and agents of the Devil." It is difficult to ascertain how the Apache reacted to this kind of proselytism, but by 1940 there were definite signs that other factors, having no connection with the missionary effort, were undermining their ceremonial system and the influence of medicine men.

For one thing, ceremonials were becoming more and more costly. As noted earlier, the major expense of any ceremonial is tied up with procuring enough food to provide all who attend with a generous meal. During aboriginal times, herds of stolen livestock and the spoils of year-round hunting provided the necessary surplus. But raiding had become a thing of the past and, with the confinement of Apaches to reservations, hunting had been limited to Government-imposed "seasons." As the native economy gave way to a system based on monetary exchange, the Apache were forced to rely more and more heavily on trading posts. Here, of course, purchases had to be made with U.S. currency or other items to which white traders attached an equivalent worth. However, money was not plentiful, and few families had personal possessions valuable enough to buy food in the quantity necessary for ceremonial feasts. No doubt, the clan system, with its network of reciprocal obligations, worked to defray the cost of ritual undertakings. But let us not forget that it was at this point in Apache history—1930 to 1940— that Grenville Goodwin observed the clan system beginning to break down.

Judging from the accounts of Apache informants born before 1915, the effects of these changes on the ceremonial system were three-fold:

1. Fewer ceremonials were given, and there was a sharp decline in ceremonials requiring more than one night to perform.

2. Ceremonials not directly concerned with curing as, for example, the girl's puberty rite, were held less and less frequently.

3. Young Apaches, anxious to become medicine men, tended to acquire only those ceremonials for which there was a steady demand, that is, curing ceremonials. Other types of ritual were not learned and, as a consequence, became destined for extinction.

Converts

In the settlement of Cibecue, it was not until the late 1930s that Apaches began to show any sustained interest in attending church. Some went out of sheer curiosity, others in hope of receiving gifts. And a significant few went because they were unhappy with the behavior of their own medicine men. Basically, the problem was alcohol—too much of it. From time to time, medicine men were getting drunk while conducting ceremonials. This development disturbed the Apache quite as much as it did the missionaries. To the latter, it merely went to prove that alcohol was "evil" and that medicine men were in league with Satan. But to Apaches, the implications were much more serious.

Long before white men set foot in Apache territory, the Indians produced a potentially intoxicating beverage known as *tuɫpai* ("grey water"). Made from corn, it is very mild and, unless consumed quickly and in large quantities, has only the slightest inebriating effects. For the most part, drinking *tuɫpai* was restricted to important social occasions, including ceremonials, when large groups of people came together for the purpose of participating in some collective enterprise. In this context, it served the useful purpose of promoting esprit de corps or, in the words of one informant, "making people feel good about each other and what they were doing together."

Placed on reservations, the Apache continued to make *tuɫpai*; but now, confused and disillusioned, they frequently drank to excess. No longer a lubricant for social relations, *tuɫpai* became an anesthetic against uncertainty and frustration. Other forms of alcohol were also available and, before the sale of liquor on the reservation was legalized in the middle 1950s, intricate bootlegging operations were set up to obtain it. As time went on, *tuɫpai* was supplemented at ceremonies with wine, beer, and whiskey.

Singing chants all night is an exhausting task, and it had long been the custom for medicine men to drink a few cups of *tuɫpai* during the course of a ceremonial to combat fatigue. Under no circumstances, however, were they supposed to get intoxicated. It is easy to see why. When drunk, a medicine man might handle improperly a piece of ritual paraphernalia, or deviate from the proper sequence of chants, or lose consciousness before the ceremonial was finished. Worst of all, he might get angry and attempt to practice witchcraft. Any one of these transgressions would nullify the ceremonial's objectives, offend the powers involved, and threaten the welfare of everyone present. In short, instead of fulfilling their basic function of restoring and affirming good relations with the realm of power, ceremonials conducted by intoxicated medicine men could only serve to make them worse.

Elderly informants recall that very few of the medicine men in Cibecue used alcohol irresponsibly. Most medicine men, they say, drank sparingly during ceremonials and several, anxious to avoid criticism and enhance their reputations, gave it up entirely. Nonetheless, a precedent had been set. And it served as both a pretext and an excuse for a small group of dissatisfied Apaches to re-evaluate the missionary effort and, in some instances, permanently align themselves with it.

Who were the people who composed this band of so-called converts, and what besides intoxicated medicine men—for surely there were other reasons— prompted them to experiment with a religious system other than their own? For the most part, they were younger people; in 1950, only a few were over twenty-five years of age. In addition, practically all had at some point attended boarding school (at Fort Apache or elsewhere) or worked for wages off the reservation. In the context of these activities, they came into protracted contact with whites and learned the rudiments of spoken English. More important, they developed a strong desire to possess some of the things the white man owned, such as pick-up trucks, electricity, sewing machines, and stoves. The problem was how to acquire them.

Money was needed in large sums and, according to the white men, was not to be wasted on drink, or shared, or given away. To the contrary, it was to be hoarded over long periods of time until enough had accumulated to make the desired purchase. But, the Apaches decided, more was involved than this. There were obvious indications that the white man had help in acquiring the things he wanted. Just as powers aided Apaches who controlled the appropriate chants, so did God and his son Jesus aid those who went to church and made requests in prayer. Of course, God and Jesus did not procure outright the items the white man wished for, but they did help him accomplish those things necessary to save money, such as getting jobs, working steadily day in and day out, not getting drunk, and resisting the demands of relatives who claimed a share of his surplus wealth. Did not the missionaries say "all good things come to those who pray?" and that God and Jesus were the source "from which all blessings flow"? And did not the missionaries own cars and have electricity?

There were other features of the white man's religion that the Apaches found attractive; for example, whereas chants and ceremonials had to be paid for, Christian prayers and church services cost nothing. God, it was understood, gave them and Himself away for free. Equally significant was the fact that, because God and Jesus were interested only in what was good for man, they would not allow themselves to be used for witchcraft. In the long run, perhaps, it might be safer to acquire God and Jesus than a power.

It should be obvious by now that, during the initial stages of their religious acculturation, few Apaches became familiar with the intricate ideological under-pinnings of Christianity; instead, they seized upon a limited number of key con-cepts—God, Jesus, prayer, and so forth—and, in accordance with their own view of the world, redefined them to suit their immediate needs. The Virgin Mary was equated with Changing Woman, and Jesus with Changing Woman's son, *nayenezgǝne* ("Slayer of Monsters"). Sorcerers and love witches were interpreted as having affinities with the devil; God and Christ, behaving much like powers, began to offer themselves to Apaches in dreams.

Faith-Healers

In the early 1950s, the majority of Apaches who went to church in Cibecue continued to participate in native ceremonials. There were any number of reasons for this, but probably the most significant was that Christianity, as the Indians understood it, made no effective provision for curing. Whatever the new religion might offer in the way of accumulating material goods or combating the excessive use of alcohol, there was nothing in it that dealt with neutralizing the effects of sicknesses caused by power. Confronted with this disparity, the partially accultur-ated Apache saw nothing incompatible about participating in both systems simul-taneously, for he perceived them to be complementary and not, as the missionaries did, diametrically opposed. One system was directed toward one set of problems, the second system to another. So long as it was possible to derive benefits from each, why restrict oneself to one system only?

Shortly before 1960, fundamentalist faith-healers appeared in Cibecue and, at a series of tent meetings, proclaimed that Jesus Christ could heal sickness of any kind. Anyone, the new missionaries said, who truly believed in Jesus could be assured of "everlasting life," but first, on the grounds that failure to do so would make both God and Jesus angry, he had to stop participating in native ceremonials. For those Apaches in Cibecue who were already marginally involved with Christianity, but who found unsatisfactory its lack of emphasis on curing, this message carried considerable importance. But even more important was the fact that several of the faith-healing preachers were themselves Western Apaches. Originally from the reservation at San Carlos, these highly acculturated individuals had recently been cured by Christ (or so they said) and had journeyed to Cibecue and other similarly isolated settlements on the Fort Apache Reservation to share with others their personal knowledge of "miracles."

Prior to the coming of the fundamentalists, almost all of what the Apaches learned about the white man's religion had been taught to them by white men. With two or three notable exceptions, the earlier missionaries spoke only English and, even when aided by native translators, experienced only measured success in communicating the ideas associated with Christianity. Now, for the first time in Apache history, these ideas—or at least that portion of them central to faith-healing—were being presented *to* Apaches *by* Apaches in a language that all Apaches could understand.

Assuming the fundamentalist preachers were not lying—and there were many Apaches in Cibecue who entertained the possibility—God and Jesus, if treated with appropriate respect, could be instrumental in producing truly remarkable cures. Moreover, since they were able to diagnose and heal without costly ceremonials, the sick and destitute were saved from spending large sums of money. The Apache faith-healers were full of stories about the miracles Jesus had performed but, as they themselves acknowledged, unless one had actually experienced or witnessed such a miracle, the benefits of Christianity would remain out of reach. The only way to secure these benefits, the missionaries said, was to turn completely from the "medicine man way" and seek help exclusively from Christ.

To a few Apaches, this formula proved so compelling that they were moved to stand up in tent meeting, and publicly declare their intention to "give up *diyin*" and "follow Jesus" instead. Significantly, most of these individuals were the converts who had flirted with Christianity in the 1940s and 1950s, who had earlier questioned the effectiveness of medicine men, and who, as Cibecue became less and less cut off from the outside world, had derived satisfaction from the progress of their own acculturation.

The majority of Apaches in Cibecue, whose orientation was more conservative, responded to the faith-healers less enthusiastically. How, they wanted to know, could the missionaries categorically deny the validity of native ceremonials? And why, in order to maintain a productive relationship with God and Jesus, should it be necessary to neglect those with black-tailed deer, snake, and bear? After all, if one violated taboos, these and other powers were still perfectly capable of making people sick. Aside from the tesimony of persons familiar with miracles, what assurance was there that God and Jesus knew how to treat illness any better than medicine men? Suppose one gave up the "medicine man way," offended a power, got sick, and then discovered that God and Jesus were unable or reluctant to perform a cure. What then? Apaches knew all too well that powers could be unpredictable and capricious. Why should God and Jesus be so different?

Today, nearly a decade after the fundamentalists first set foot in Cibecue, the old ceremonial system persists. But it has been weakened. As a consequence of investing God and Jesus with the attributes of powers, by extolling these deities' miraculous abilities and ready accessibility, and by ceaselessly denying the validity of traditional ritual, the faith-healers have managed to persuade a number of Apaches that the old system may be deficient.

Christian Ritual

For most Apaches, the decision to embrace Christianity depends only in part upon reconciling the ideological discrepancies discussed above. Typically, other considerations come into play. Primary among these are (1) the individual's reaction to Christian ritual (by no means always favorable); and (2) his willingness to confront the interpersonal problems that are likely to arise once he assumes the role of convert (*inošut*). Let us consider these factors in relation to the experiences of two Apaches who, although exposed to Christianity under essentially the same conditions, responded to it in very different ways.

James L., aged forty-eight, was born in Cibecue and, except for two years of ranch work off the reservation, spent his entire life there. As a child, he attended numerous ceremonials, some of which were conducted by his father's brother who was a medicine man. James' mother, an old woman and an influential member of a large clan, had no doubts whatever about the effectiveness of ceremonialism and was angry and impatient with those of her relatives who joined forces with the missionaries. She was especially unhappy with James' younger brother who had fallen into the annoying habit of proclaiming himself, when drunk, a Lutheran.

As an adult, James watched the missionary activity in Cibecue with detached curiousity. He was interested in what his friends said about the white man's religion and admitted that it contained certain elements which sounded attractive. At one point, around 1955, he was persuaded to attend Lutheran and Catholic services, but he was not favorably impressed. James found Christian ritual to be bland, sterile, and uninteresting. However strongly it might appeal to white men, he decided, it lacked ingredients of vital importance to him.

Whereas the vast majority of Apache ceremonials take place at night and last for hours, Christian services are daytime affairs and, by comparison, extremely brief. This runs counter to the Apache belief that powers should be given ample time to work and, especially when invoked to aid in cures, respond most effectively in the dark. Said James L.: "Those missionaries get together and want to hurry up. They want you to just sit there and listen to what they say and go away when they are done talking. I don't see how they can get Jesus to do much that way."

This observation points to what Apaches consider another shortcoming of Christian ritual, namely that it does not provide adequate opportunity for individual participation. At native ceremonials there is always plenty to do, and no one is ever compelled to "just sit there." Prior to a ceremony, men can help out by hauling firewood, procuring items of ritual paraphernalia, and transporting people to the dance-ground. Women aid in the preparation of food, tend one another's children and, if they are old and experienced, give speeches on proper conduct. During the actual proceedings, men are encouraged to join with the medicine man in singing, make pollen blessings, and act as substitute drummers. Always there is dancing, either singly, or, as is most often the case, in long lines formed by the dancers linking arms.

The structure and organization of an Apache ceremonial is such that anyone who attends can take part and, in some way or other, contribute actively to its successful performance. This is accompanied by a feeling of inclusion and personal involvement that Christian ritual does not supply. At native ceremonials the Apache is engaged as an active participant; in church he is isolated as an idle spectator.

There is also the complaint that, except for fundamentalist tent meetings, the mood of Christian ritual is uncomfortably somber. "At church," says James L., "they want you to be quiet and look serious, like maybe you were afraid of something." It is true that at Apache ceremonials one sees little of the pious restraint which typifies the behavior of white churchgoers. To the contrary, even at the most potent curing rituals the atmosphere is one of heightened animation. Children race about wildly and keep up a steady stream of high-pitched chatter. Adults, some in search of alcohol, move freely through the crowd, visiting with friends and relatives and shouting mock criticisms at dancers with awkward style. Over the sound of the drums, there is laughter and the hum of conversation.

Let us recall that at all ceremonials Apaches are enjoined to "have happiness" in their minds and to "think good thoughts," these being the conditions under which powers are supposed to work best. To appear serious or withdrawn is inappropriate because it conveys the impression of sadness and, by extension, a disregard for the ceremony's successful outcome. This is the way Apaches interpret much of the behavior they see in church, and they find it both mystifying and disturbing.

There is yet another feature of missionary services which people like James L. find unpleasant, and this is the condescending and sometimes insulting nature of sermons. Said one Apache: "I guess they (missionaries) don't think we know anything about what's right. A lot of what they tell us is O.K., but our people knew that a long time before they came."

Apaches do not object in principle to being instructed and advised in matters pertaining to moral conduct; indeed, as we have seen, speeches on the importance of good behavior are an integral part of every major ceremonial. What they dislike is being addressed as if they were children, for this implies what they know is not true, i.e., that they are incapable of distinguishing right from wrong, good from bad. In assuming that the Apache is either unable or reluctant to make mature decisions in the sphere of personal ethics, missionaries insult his character and intelligence and, as a result, often engender considerable resentment.

The foregoing remarks apply most directly to the older, more established missionary groups in Cibecue: the Lutherans, Catholics, and Mormons. The ritual of the faith-healers warrants separate treatment because it is considerably less staid, and Apaches respond to it in a characteristically different fashion.

In several respects, fundamentalist tent meetings bear a close formal resemblance to native ceremonials. They begin at dusk and usually continue long into the night. There is loud music (usually provided by highly amplified electric guitars), much singing and, for those who "feel the spirit of Jesus," ample room to dance. Members of the congregation are permitted to converse with each other, eat, and step outside whenever they wish. They are also encouraged to participate by responding verbally to sermons, which they do with shouts of "thank you Jesus," "hallelujah," and "praise God." Sometimes, the enthusiasm generated by tent meetings gets out of hand. On one occasion, an Apache girl, dancing wildly, struck her head on a post, sank to the ground, and was nearly trampled by other dancers. Later the same evening, a young mother tripped, apparently in trance. Her skirts flew up as she fell, and for several moments she lay motionless, naked from the waist down.

Incidents of this sort provoke sharp criticism. Too much of fundamentalist ritual, Apaches observe, is aimed at getting people so excited that they abandon their composure and lose control. This is understandable (though by no means considered attractive) in adolescents who do not yet comprehend fully the implications of reserve and restraint. But among adults, who interpret the absence of these qualities as indicative of a lack of self-esteem, it is considered undignified and degrading. James L. commented as follows:

> Some people go crazy at those miracle dances. They dance around like they don't see nothing and roll on the ground and shake around. They don't know what they're doing, so they don't care if anybody sees them that way . . . it looks funny to these older people around here, like maybe the ones who do it have lost their thinking . . . lots of people around here don't like it. It looks bad. . . . Those miracle missionaries can make people do those things and, after, when they think about it they get ashamed of what they did. That's why a lot of people stay away.

In this section we have attempted to show that the Apache's evaluation of Christianity may be influenced to a significant degree by his reaction to missionary ritual. Where this reaction is unfavorable, as in the case of James L., it strengthens the appeal of native ceremonialism and, concomitantly, mitigates against conversion.

The Price of Conversion

The Apache becomes a Christian at no small sacrifice to himself, for in assuming the role of convert, he must neglect certain others with which it conflicts. This disturbs profoundly his relationships with kinsmen and friends, and those who are skeptical of missionaries may retaliate with intense criticism and the threat of ostracism. In some cases, the pressure becomes unbearable and, for reasons that have nothing to do with religious ideology, the convert rejects Christianity and vows never to take it seriously again.

So it was with John D., a man of thirty-two, whose wife was cured of chronic headaches by a faith-healer in 1963. Earlier, John had arranged several ceremonials for his wife but, as he put it, "the medicine men couldn't do anything." Understandably impressed with the faith-healer's cure, John and his wife decided to attend tent meetings more often. Within a few months, John's wife was firmly convinced that she ought to "be with Jesus." John himself was less certain.

In the summer of 1964, John developed pain and numbness in his left arm and went to a medicine man for diagnosis. A curing ceremonial was prescribed but, at his wife's insistence, John agreed first to seek aid from faith-healers. He attended tent meetings on two consecutive nights and discovered, midway through the second, that the pain in his arm was gone. A few days later, having cancelled the ceremonial, John announced he would "give up medicine men."

This decision was to have ramifications that John had not anticipated. As a "good Christian," he learned, he would have to give up drinking beer and *tułpai* with his male friends. In addition, he could no longer go to rodeos, fairs, or movies; these activities were "sinful" because, according to the faith-healers, they fostered illicit sexual behavior and took one's mind off Jesus. Before his conversion, John had frequently helped prepare ritual paraphernalia for ceremonials but now, of course, this too was forbidden. Likewise, it would make God angry if John contributed money to ceremonials, or supplied food, or loaned out his collection of eagle feathers.

As time went on, the sphere of John's activities became increasingly restricted; there were fewer and fewer things he could do. Aside from going to work, and making a weekly trip off the reservation for groceries, he spent practically all of his time at home. John noticed that his friends were visiting him less frequently, and his wife's sister reported that he was being accused in gossip of "looking out only for himself."

This was the issue when John's maternal parallel cousin arrived at his camp one day and, having explained that his daughter was ill and needed ceremonial treatment, requested money to hire a medicine man. John refused, whereupon his cousin became violently angry. As John recalls the scene:

> He sure yelled at me, all bad things. . . . He just stood there and wouldn't stop. "I don't know what you want to be this way for. You have always helped me out but now you won't do it. Some people told me not to come here, they knew you wouldn't give me money, but I didn't believe them. You always helped me out before. You think you are better than us because you are *inošut* (convert), and you have turned away from your close relatives. . . . Well, if you aren't going to help us out, maybe you won't be able to come to us anymore."

Word of John's refusal to aid his cousin spread quickly through Cibecue, and within a few days he was being criticized even more harshly than before. John was unhappy and distracted.

I heard about it—those people talking bad about me. Always before, I get along real good with my close relatives. Now they're all saying bad things about me. My wife said just not to listen to what they said. But I knew they were angry because of what I did to my relative.

In the weeks that followed, John stopped going to tent meetings. And about a month after the incident with his cousin he attended a curing ceremonial and, together with several of his kinsmen, got very drunk. Afterwards, his wife berated him and warned that unless he changed his ways God would punish him. John acknowledged that this was indeed a possibility but said, regardless, he had no intention of continuing on as an *inošut*. Explaining his decision, John said simply: "I just thought about it and thought that medicine men were good after all." John's brother had another explanation which, all things considered, is probably more accurate. Said he:

My brother got worried about what people were saying about him. He knew they were mad because he wouldn't help them out. . . . So he thought about it and just went back to the way he was before.

As a rule, most Apache converts do not adhere to the restrictions imposed upon them as assiduously as John D. Responding alternately to the injunctions of missionaries and the criticism of friends and relatives, they shift from one extreme to the other in search of a workable compromise. This vacillation is symptomatic of an attempt to avoid the disruptive consequences that total conversion would produce. As we have seen, strict conformity to the Christian ideal—at least as it is presented by the missionaries in Cibecue—excludes the Apache from activities to which he has grown accustomed and from which he derives enjoyment and satisfaction. By the same token, it conflicts sharply with traditional standards for the conduct of interpersonal relationships and the fulfillment of critical kinship obligations. Under these circumstances, it is very difficult to be a "good Christian" and a good Apache at the same time.

It should be emphasized, however, that for Apaches who are able to find a solution to this dilemma—and still retain their commitment to Christianity—the new religion can provide substantial benefits. There is no doubt, for example, that it has helped several individuals overcome serious drinking problems, a step forward which enabled them to secure steady employment and raise significantly their standard of living. A few Apaches maintain that their fear of ghosts and witches has subsided as a consequence of their decision to "follow Jesus," and among others—bent upon acculturation and anxious to identify closely with whites—becoming a Christian is regarded as a positive achievement.

Still, for the majority of Apaches in Cibecue the new religion leaves much to be desired. As an ideology, it leaves important questions unanswered; as a body of ritual, it is deficient in many ways; and finally, as a code for the conduct of human relationships, it often creates problems. In these times of rapidly accelerating change, few adult Apaches in Cibecue would claim that the way of the medicine man is in all respects superior. But neither would they claim to have found anything to adequately take its place.

Glossary

English Terms

AFFINAL RELATIVES: Kinsmen who trace relationship to one another through at least one marital link.

BILATERAL DESCENT: A nonunilineal principle of descent by which all consanguineal relatives are recognized as kinsmen.

CONSANGUINEAL RELATIVES: Persons who are genetically related; that is, who trace relationship to one another on the basis of biological descent.

CROSS-COUSIN: Father's sister's children; mother's brother's children.

ENDOGAMY: A regulation which requires that an individual marry within a defined social group; such a group, that is one whose members are permitted to marry, is *endogamous*.

EXOGAMY: A regulation which requires that an individual marry "outside" a defined social group; such a group, that is, one whose members are not allowed to marry is *exogamous*.

FRATERNAL JOINT FAMILY: Typically composed of two or more coresident brothers, their wives and children.

LEVIRATE: The marriage of a woman to her deceased husband's brother.

LINEAGE: A unilineal consanguineal kinship group whose members can actually trace their mutual relationship from a common ancestor.

MATRILINEAL DESCENT: A type of unilineal descent by which relationship is traced through females only.

MATRILOCAL EXTENDED FAMILY: Typically composed of a woman, her husband, their unmarried children, their married daughters, and the latter's husbands and children.

MATRILOCAL RESIDENCE: A type of post-marital residence in which the newly wedded couple establishes a household with (or in the area of) the wife's parents.

NONRESIDENTIAL KIN GROUP: A kinship group whose members are spatially dispersed (for example, the Western Apache clan).

NUCLEAR FAMILY: A kinship group composed of a man, his wife, and their children.

PARALLEL COUSIN: Father's brother's children; mother's sister's children.

POLYGYNY: The marriage of one man to two or more woman at the same time.

RESIDENTIAL KIN GROUP: A spatially localized kinship group; that is, one whose members live together in the same place (for example, the Western Apache *gota*).

SIBLING: Brother or sister.

SORORAL JOINT FAMILY: Typically composed of two or more coresident sisters, their husbands and their children.

SORORATE: The marriage of a man to his deceased wife's sister.

Apache Terms

destsǫ: Objects which are either immobile or which depend for movement upon the intervention of outside forces.

diyi?: Supernatural "power(s)"; this term is also frequently used to designate chants (*si*).

diyin: Person(s) who "owns" a supernatural power: includes medicine men, sorcerers, and love witches.

edotaɫ: Diagnostic ceremonial(s), usually terminating at midnight.

godistso: "love magic"; a technique of love witches.

godiyo: Category of objects considered "holy" by the Western Apache.

gojitaɫ: Curing ceremonial(s), generally lasting throughout the night.

gota: A basic unit of Western Apache social organization, usually (but not necessarily) corresponding to a matrilocal extended family.

gową: The occupants and location of a single nuclear household.

hatiʔi: Clan; more specifically those clan members who live together in the same settlement.

hinda: Objects capable of generating and sustaining their own locomotive movement; includes man.

iɫkašn: "Sorcerer."

inošut: Missionary; convert.

istsənadlęžę: "Changing Woman"; a central figure in Western Apache mythology who is personified in the girl's puberty ceremonial.

naiʔes: Girl's puberty ceremonial; literally: "preparing her" or "getting her ready."

naiɫʔesn: "Sponsor"; an important role in the girl's puberty ceremonial.

odiʔi: "love witch."

šitike: Set of reciprocal obligations, cemented by girl's puberty ceremonial, between sponsor (and the members of her clan) and the pubescent girl (and the members of her clan).

References

BASSO, KEITH H., 1966. The Gift of Changing Woman. *Bulletin of the Bureau of American Ethnology*, No. 196. Washington, D. C.: Smithsonian Institution.

————, 1969. Western Apache Witchcraft. *Anthropological Papers of the University of Arizona*, No. 15, Tucson: University of Arizona Press.

————, n.d. *Kinship, Authority, and Acculturation*. Unpublished manuscript. Stanford, California.: Stanford University.

BOURKE, J. G., 1892. The Medicine Men of the Apache. *Annual Report of the Bureau of American Ethnology*, No. 9:451–595. Washington, D. C.: Smithsonian Institution.

GETTY, HARRY T., 1964. Changes in Land Use among the Western Apaches. In *Indian and Spanish American Adjustments to Arid and Semiarid Environments*, Clark S. Knowlton, editor. Lubbock: The Committee on Desert and Arid Zone Research, Contribution No. 7.

GODDARD, PLINY E., 1919. Myths and Tales from the White Mountain Apache. *Anthropological Publications of the American Museum of Natural History*, No. 24. New York: American Museum of Natural History.

————, 1920. White Mountain Apache Texts. *Anthropological Publications of the American Museum of Natural History*, No. 24. New York: American Museum of Natural History.

GOODWIN, GRENVILLIE, 1935. The Social Divisions and Economic Life of the Western Apache. *American Anthropologist* 37:55–64.

————, 1937. The Characteristics and Function of Clan in a Southern Athapaskan Culture. *American Anthropologist* 39:394–407.

————, 1938. White Mountain Apache Religion. *American Anthropologist* 40:24–37.

————, 1939. Myths and Tales of the White Mountain Apache. *Memoir No. 39*, American Folklore Society.

————, 1942. *The Social Organization of the Western Apache*. Chicago: University of Chicago Press.

————, and CHARLES R. KAUT, 1954. A Native Religious Movement among the White Mountain and Cibecue Apache. *Southwestern Journal of Anthropology* 10:385–404.

————, and CLYDE KLUCKHOHN, 1945. A Comparison of Navaho and White Mountain Ceremonial Forms and Categories. *Southwestern Journal of Anthropology* 1:498–506.

KAUT, CHARLES R., 1957. The Western Apache Clan System: Its Origins and Development. *University of New Mexico Publications in Anthropology*, No. 9. Albuquerque: University of New Mexico.

KLUCKHOHN, CLYDE, 1944. *Navaho Witchcraft*. Boston: The Beacon Press.

LINTON, RALPH, 1945. *The Cultural Background of Personality*. New York: Appleton-Century-Crofts.

LOWIE, ROBERT, 1947. *Primitive Society*. New York: Liveright.

MALINOWSKI, BRONISLAW, 1931. Culture. In *Encyclopedia of the Social Sciences*, Vol. 4, New York.

POSPISIL, LEOPOLD, 1964. Law and Societal Structure Among the Nunamiut Eskimo. In *Explorations in Cultural Anthropology*, Ward H. Goodenough, editor. New York: McGraw-Hill Book Company.

REAGAN, ALBERT, 1930. Notes on the Indians of the Fort Apache Region. *Anthropological Publications of the American Museum of Natural History*, No. 31. New York: American Museum of Natural History.

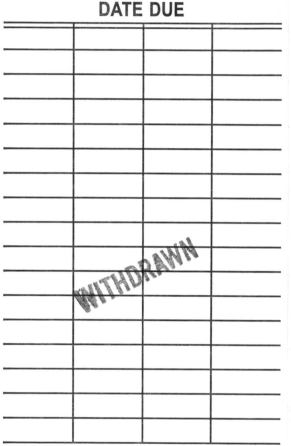

DATE DUE

DEMCO 38-296

Please remember that this is a library book, and that it belongs only temporarily to each person who uses it. Be considerate. Do not write in this, or any, library book.